INSURANCE SETTLEMENT SECRET$

Legal Notice

The information contained in this book does not constitute legal advice. As legal advice must be tailored to the specific circumstances of each case, and laws are constantly changing, nothing provided herein should be used as a substitute for the advice of competent counsel.

ISBN-10: 1551806908
ISBN-13: 978-1551806907

Netserf Media
Title: Insurance Settlement Secrets
Author: Matheson MacKinnon, B.A., LL.B
www.insurancesettlementsecrets.org
info@insurancesettlementsecrets.org

INSURANCE SETTLEMENT SECRET$

Step By Step Guide to Get
THOUSANDS of DOLLARS
More for Your Auto Accident
Injury without a LAWYER!

Matheson MacKinnon B.A., LL.B.

Table of Contents

Claims Forms Kit

Introduction

Why *Insurance Settlement Secrets* is such a great Investment for You:

Congratulations on your purchase of *Insurance Settlement Secrets!*

You now have in your possession pure inside information that I have learned from years of experience in the legal world and the Insurance industry handling, negotiating and settling injury claims.

This book and the Insurance Settlement Secrets revealed come directly from within the Insurance Industry. It is a behind the scenes look at how the Insurance Companies process automobile accident injury claims.

Once you read and absorb the information in this book you will know more about your auto accident injury claim than even the Insurance Companies you will be dealing with.

This book is written in straightforward plain English. Instead of trying to impress you and intimidate you on the complexity of the issues involved, I have distilled the whole accident injury claims process into 3 clear and simple stages.

This benefits you because not only is ***knowledge power*** but also ***clarity is power.***

When you have finished reading this book the mystery of the injury claims process will be gone and the inside knowledge that you will gain will give you very ***real leverage*** when negotiating with the Insurance Company.

This ***leverage*** will translate into thousands of dollars more in your pocket than if you pursued your claim without this information.

How can you benefit the most from this book?

You can benefit most from this book if you read it before or just after you have been in an automobile accident. This is because what you do immediately after the accident is very important in the success of your injury claim.

Remember, what you have paid for here is **exclusive Information** that is not known by the general public and is worth thousands of dollars to you in the claims process, just by having this knowledge.

The Scope of this book:

What you are about to learn is from an Insurance Industry Insider who has worked for years and negotiated hundreds and hundreds injury settlements.

You are about to learn:

1. The steps you must take when you are injured in a motor vehicle accident.

2. The Key Elements of the Claims process and the players involved.

3. How to deal with the Insurance Company when they call.

4. Learn how to have the advantage against the Insurance Company.

5. Learn what medical information is crucial to your claim.

6. Learn to push the same buttons that you would pay an experienced lawyer to do. You can do this for free!

7. Learn about *"Whiplash"* and *"Soft tissue"* injuries.

8. When to start negotiating the settlement.

9. The *"Achilles heel"* of insurance companies.

10. How to successfully negotiate the settlement of your injury claim for thousands more than you could without the aid of Insurance Settlement Secrets information.

11. Inside tips about how to approach hiring personal injury lawyers should you require their services as a last resort.

This book deals with how to pursue a claim for injuries arising from **automobile accidents.** However, the principles can be applied to other types of injury claims, such as "slip and fall" injury claims and Worker's Compensation injury claims.

This book will guide you through the process and will reveal to you Insurance Settlement Secrets on what Red Flags you should watch for and when you should seek legal representation.

What you are about to learn is *not legal advice*. It is insider information on *How Insurance Companies Process Auto Accident Injury claims*.

That's right! You are going to learn in detail what the Insurance Companies do not want you to know.

Why? Because, by knowing this inside information they can no longer earn thousands of dollars of profits from you.

There is a place for personal injury lawyers. You will need to consult a personal injury lawyer where your *injury is more serious* with long term consequences or if your claim involves *real legal issues.*

If you still wish to consult a lawyer for legal advice you should do so.

However, you should do so only after having read this book. Then you can approach a lawyer from an informed position.

Again, simply having the *Insurance Settlement Secrets* knowledge will put you at a huge advantage when dealing with the Insurance

Companies as well as saving you thousands of dollars in legal fees.

Insurance Settlement Secrets will guide you through the process and each of the **key stages** of the insurance claims process.

You will be guided through **exact steps** you must take. Don't worry, you will not have to do a lot of extra work. These are the **same steps** you would have to take even if you hired the best high-priced lawyer.

In this book I will also give you real ***Exclusive Information*** from ***Inside the Insurance Company*** that you are claiming against.

I have this information gained from working for years settling personal Injury claims arising out of Automobile accidents.

That's right, I was the person that had the final authority on how much the claim was worth and who actually issued the settlement check to the injured claimant.

At any time I had millions of dollars in my authority to spend on injury claim settlements.

Once you have completed the necessary steps following your automobile accident, your claim will be ***"bullet proof".*** This means that the Insurance Company **cannot deny your claim**.

You will also learn how to negotiate just like an expert in insurance claims. You will learn how to use leverage against the insurance company to maximize your injury settlement, resulting in thousands of dollars more for you.

This book will guide you through the settlement process for what the Insurance Industry considers **"Small"** claims. However, what the Insurance Industry considers "Small" claims is far from peanuts to you or me. Read on to discover how many thousands of dollars we are talking about.

Let's get started!

The Big Picture

In Automobile Accident Injuries there are **only 3 things** that must be demonstrated. The 3 things you must show are:

1. That the <u>other driver</u> was the CAUSE (or was the <u>main</u> cause) of the motor vehicle accident.

2. That you suffered an INJURY as a RESULT OF THE ACCIDENT.

3. The SERIOUSNESS OF YOUR INJURY and LOSS.

These three elements do not have to be proven. They simply have to be **reasonably certain** to convince the Insurance Company it is not worth contesting these facts in court.

You will learn real Insurance Settlement Secrets how you won't have to actually prove any of these things, and in fact both <u>your Insurance Company</u> and the <u>other driver's Insurance Company</u> will **do** this for you.

The CLAIMS PROCESS is very simple. It is not rocket science. All you have to do is open your CLAIMS and take care of yourself and get medical help.

This book is packed with detailed information on how the claims process works when you are injured in a motor vehicle accident.

In order that you do not become overwhelmed you need to step back and look at the big picture first. This is to show you where all this information leads and to take away anxiety.

The Motor Vehicle Accident Injury claims process can be divided into 3 clear stages: **Stage 1, Stage 2** and **Stage 3**.

At each stage there are a **sequence of steps** you must take. It is important that you complete each stage before moving on to the next.

At all times you must be clear of exactly where you are in the claims process as **timing** is very important. If you take action too late or too early it can have **serious consequences** to the outcome of your claim.

In order to make the process even easier for you I have illustrated each stage using traffic lights as symbols.

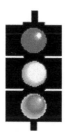

If you can read traffic lights you will have no problem getting through the injury claims process against the Insurance Companies and successfully negotiating your injury settlement for thousands of dollars more than you would without this information, even if you had a lawyer.

The following are the 3 basic stages of the Injury Claims Process:

Stage 1   **Motor Vehicle Accident**

Stage 2   **Rehabilitation**

Stage 3   **Negotiation**

At each stage there is a sequence of steps you must take. They fall under the following general headings.

Stage   **Motor Vehicle Accident**

-Getting Immediate Medical Attention
-Notification of Motor Vehicle Accident to your Insurance Company
-Opening Different Insurance Claims
-Establishing Liability

Stage   **Rehabilitation**

-Following Through with Medical Treatment
-Recording and Documenting
-Monitoring your Legal Options

Stage ③   **Negotiation**

- Putting Together Your Evidence
- Calculating the Value of Your Injury Claim
- Negotiating Settlement

At the end of this book is a <u>Claims Forms and Sample Letter kit,</u> and these are all color coded to make this process as simple as possible.

If you follow through with the steps at each stage you will convince the At-Fault Driver's Insurance Company of the 3 things necessary to make your claim *"bullet proof"* and guarantee that you will receive **maximum settlement** for your injury claim.

Organization and knowing exactly what to do and when to do it will make the difference of thousands of dollars in your injury settlement. Also, simply knowing what is happening through each step will take away anxiety and stress for you.

Stage 1

The Motor Vehicle Accident

Okay, you are driving along, minding your own business or maybe you are stopped at an intersection when *"bang"* you are hit from behind. This is called a "rear-end" collision. Or someone goes through the red light and hits you broadside, i.e. *"T-bones"* your vehicle.

First you are in shock. You are stunned and shaken up. Thoughts run through your head. What happened? Where am I?

Even if its just a minor accident, these impacts can be very disorienting. You freeze for you don't know how long. There are honking horns. Cars are trying to pass. You may have passengers, or children. Are they okay?

The air bags may have deployed and hit you in the face. Ouch! The horn may be stuck on.

You look around or in the rear mirror. If you were hit in the rear you typically freeze for a short period of time, your hands holding tightly to the steering wheel. You brain is trying to assess what has happened. It can be very traumatic. You may be in a state of shock.

Then you start coming around. Am I hurt? Is anybody hurt? What about the car? Was that my fault? What about my appointment? How will I get to work? How much will it cost to get the car fixed? What about the other car and driver?

You get out of your car finally, slowly and carefully. Other cars are whizzing past. You see the other driver. You both look at the damage.

You are not sure what happened. It appears the other driver was at fault and caused the accident but you may start to doubt yourself. Was that light really green? Was I supposed to go?

The other driver may not say anything or may offer to pay for the damages saying *"It's only a little scratch"*.

The other driver may be aggressive and hostile and point the blame at you.

You (or the other driver) call the police on a cell phone. If you do call the police, the dispatch voice may ask you if you are injured.

Typically many injured people are in shock and say "I think I'm okay. I'm fine." This is natural. Most people try and put on a brave face in the stress of the situation, and with the traffic and the cars in the middle of the road.

Insurance Settlement Secret # 1

Often the police won't come if no one is injured and the accident appears minor. However, just because the police to do not come, does not mean that you are not injured or that this is automatically a minor claim.

In this case you and the other driver may be able to drive away from the situation after exchanging Insurance and Contact information. You are in a daze as you drive away.

If the impact is significant you may not be able to move the vehicles, and a tow truck will be called. Your vehicle may put in a storage yard. The damages to the vehicle may make it not worth repairing and it would be declared a *"total loss"*.

You may not be aware you are injured. Like most people, you are not thinking about yourself at this point. You may be thinking about your job or your vehicle damage.

How will you get to work without your vehicle? What about the kids?

What will it cost? You are probably in a mild to moderate state of shock. Your heart is racing.

Stressful! And this is just the start.

So there you are, standing beside your damaged automobile. You've exchanged Insurance and Contact information with the other driver.

Depending on the seriousness of the accident the Police may have been to the scene. If the Police do come to the scene, they will question you and the other driver, any passengers and possible witnesses.

If you are visibly and obviously injured with cuts bruises fractures etc., an ambulance may be called to take you to the Hospital Emergency.

But what if, as in the majority of minor accidents, you outwardly appear fine. You can walk without aid. You have no obvious injuries. No cuts and bruises.

Like most people, you will probably put on a brave face and say *"I'm Okay"*. Especially men, who as a matter of pride will not admit to a little pain.

Like most people, if your car is drivable, you will want to go straight home. If the car is not drivable, you may have a family member or friend come and drive you home.

Many people, when they get home will first call their employer and advise that they have been in an accident and request the rest of the day off.

Most employers will say okay but expect you back at work the next day.

Like many working people you are anxious about your job, your mortgage, your car payments and bills etc.

15

In my experience, you would be surprised how many people after an accident, even though they are sore or in pain, will try hard to work through it and get to work the next day out of fear of losing their jobs.

For most ordinary hardworking Americans and Canadians this is the reality.

Many people have private health insurance through their employer or HMO. Many others do <u>not</u>.

If you are self employed, you may feel especially vulnerable and may not have any coverage. Self employed people also have to keep their business running and may have difficulty taking any down time.

Many young people and students may not have adequate health coverage. They may be in the middle of exams or also have a part time job.

Therefore, if you have little or no private health coverage you will likely not want to make a fuss and will grin and bear the pain and stiffness and go back to work as if nothing happened. You may be more concerned about getting your car fixed.

Insurance Settlement Secret # 2

The <u>Insurance Companies</u> stand to **profit** considerably from your willingness to downplay your accident and injury.

But have no fear! Take a Deep Breath.

I am here to guide you through every step of the way so that you can maximize your injury settlement and make sure the Insurance Companies and lawyers **do not profit** at your expense.

No Insurance Company can take advantage of you if you have the **right information**, especially Insider information on how the Insurance Injury Claims process works.

The Key is Knowledge

Read on. You will have all the Inside Information you need to claim and successfully negotiate your injury settlement for thousands of dollars more in your pocket than even if you hired a top lawyer.

The Players in a Motor Vehicle Accident

Insurance Settlement Secret # 3

As soon you are injured in an accident, whether it was your fault or not, **you become a source of income for a whole lot of people.**

That's right!

1. The **Police Officers**: They will get a fee for a copy of their report.

2. The **Tow Truck company**

3. The **Storage Yard**

4. The **Appraiser** who appraises your vehicle.

5. The **Repair Shop (Body shop)**

6. Insurance Company **Staff Claim's Adjusters** from your Insurance Company and the at-fault driver's Insurance Company.

That's just for the vehicle damages. If you are injured...

7. **The Ambulance driver**

8. The **Emergency Department at the Hospital.**
   (They also get paid for copy of Emergency Record.)

9. **Independent Adjusters** may meet with you for statements and may take photos of your vehicle damages or the accident scene to determine liability.

10. If fraud is suspected, **Private Investigators** may be hired to do video surveillance.

11. **Medical Doctors**

12. **Chiropractors, Physiotherapy Clinics or Massage Clinics**

13. **Personal Injury Lawyers**

    Personal Injury Lawyers for you or Defense Counsel for the Insurance Companies.

Finally, let's not forget:

14. **Insurance Companies**

The **Insurance Companies** also will **profit** by thousands of dollars if they can get you to sign a <u>Final Release</u> for less than your claim is really worth.

As you can see, there are lot of people who have an economic stake in the fact that you were injured in an automobile accident.

With so many players involved it is important that you keep track of who you are dealing with and that you are ***organized***.

Immediate Steps You Must Take!

Insurance Settlement Secret # 4

The **first few days** after the accident are the most important!

What you do in the first few days to a week following your motor vehicle accident can make the difference in thousands of dollars in your injury settlement.

Step #1: The action you MUST take immediately after an accident is Go to the Hospital Emergency.

If you didn't go straight to the Hospital Emergency because you had no outward signs of injury or because you didn't immediately feel any pain, or you had some pain but had other important things on your mind, **do so immediately**, either the same day or within a day or two after the accident. The **sooner the better.**

Why is it important to go to the Hospital Emergency? Why can't you wait for an appointment with your family doctor?

Three reasons:

1. You can go to the Hospital **immediately**. You don't need an appointment.

2. The sooner you seek medical attention after an accident the stronger the **causal connection** between your injury and the accident. This is extremely important for later proving your case against the Insurance Company.

3. By going to the Emergency you are getting an **Independent Medical Opinion** from a doctor who is not your family doctor. This will strengthen your claim right from the start.

Insurance Settlement Tip #1

Even though you believe you are not injured you should still go to the Hospital to get checked out. This is because some injuries, like soft tissue injuries, may appear mild at the start and then a few days or weeks later develop into something much worse.

Some types of soft tissue injuries to the neck and back are not outwardly visible but can result in very painful disabilities.

These types of injuries are very common with automobile accidents. Yet many people try and grin and bear it or shake off stiffness or pain only to have it become worse later on. It is better to be safe than sorry.

Insurance Settlement Tip # 2:

Even if you have no Health Insurance coverage and have to borrow the money to pay $50-100 for the Emergency visit, do it. This is an investment and will be worth a minimum of $1000 -$2500 whether or not you are injured.

Step 2: Make an appointment and follow up with your family doctor.

> Follow up with your family doctor. Why is this so important?

Insurance Settlement Secret # 5

The success of your claim can be summed up in one word:

"DOCUMENTS "

Almost all personal injury claims are based and valued on **documentation only**.

In the majority of cases the Insurance Company Injury Examiner, who will review your file and issue the settlement check, will **never meet with you in person**.

The only way the Insurance Injury Examiner can assess the value of the claim is by what you say over the phone and through **medical documentation**.

Therefore, if you have gone to the Emergency soon after the accident, a report called an **Emergency Record** can be ordered from the hospital.

Why is this important to you? This is important to you for two reasons:

1. When you make a claim against the At-Fault driver's Insurance Company and indicate you are injured, you will need to provide some sort of **documentary evidence of injury.**

Once the injury examiner knows that you have been to the Hospital Emergency, he or she knows that a **report can be ordered.**

No matter how mild your injury the Examiner knows he or she cannot dismiss your claim. Your claim now has real proof.

2. The Injury Examiner can now put a dollar value on your injury. With just one medical report form the Hospital Emergency, your claim is worth thousands of dollars more than a claim with no medical reports.

Insurance Settlement's Secret # 6

It would be wise for you to keep a **log** of all your contact times and dates of contact with the injury adjuster as well as doctor's visits, physiotherapy treatments, etc.

Insurance Settlement Tip # 3

See the Claims Forms Kit at the end of this book with specially designed Medical Treatment Logs for you to use for recording the exact information you need.

Insurance Settlement Tip # 4

Keep receipts of all expenses associated with treatment, including if you have to pay for housekeeping help or cab fares to clinics, etc. Receipts are proof.

These two steps: Going to the <u>Hospital Emergency</u> immediately after the accident for check up and <u>Making a follow up appointment with your Family Doctor</u> will be crucial to the later success of your injury claim.

Many people are shaken up after an accident and all they want to do is take the day off and rest or lie in bed. Rest is important but rest at home will not be much help to you when presenting your claim.

If and when you decide to pursue a claim you will have something clear and substantive on which to base the claim.

Do these 2 steps and you are off to a good start.

Remember, the purpose of this book is to show you how to make your Injury Claim *"Bullet Proof"* so that the At-Fault Driver's Insurance Company cannot deny your claim.

Different Types of Claims

When you are involved in an accident, and you are injured, you will likely have to open **not just one claim**, but <u>**several different types of claims all at the same time.**</u>

1. Property (Vehicle) Damage Claims

If you have Collision Coverage under your own Insurance Policy then your insurer will pay you directly for the damages to your vehicle.

Your Insurance company will then seek to be reimbursed from the other driver's Insurance Company, if the other driver was at fault. This is called the *"Right of Subrogation"* in the Insurance industry.

If you don't have collision coverage under your own policy then you will have to open a claim for vehicle damages against the at-fault driver's Insurance Company.

2. Medical Payments Claims

This type of claim is to cover your immediate Medical Expenses while your Injury Claim against the At-Fault driver, which can take months or years, runs its course.

A claim for Medical Payments is made against <u>your own Insurance Company</u> under <u>your Insurance policy</u> if you have coverage.

You may have several sources to claim from for medical payments.

You may have **Private Health and Disability coverage**, through your **HMO**, or **coverage through your Employer** and you may also be able to claim the shortfall of these benefits under your own automobile insurance policy.

Almost half the States in the U.S.A. have some form of **Personal Injury Protection (PIP)** coverage.

A claim for Medical Payments and expenses will likely have a certain limit.

In some states under some policies you may be required to pay this back out of any settlement you receive from a Third Party Liability claim.

You will learn in the sections on <u>Paying for Medical Treatment</u> and <u>Negotiating Your Settlement,</u> how to deal with this.

3. (Third Party) Liability Claims

If you have been injured in an automobile accident which was caused or mainly caused by another driver you can claim against his or her Insurance Company for Damages.

Insurance Settlement Secrets deals mainly with # 3, <u>Liability Claims.</u>

This is where the money is.

It is very important that you understand these different types of claims which all may be going on at the same time.

This is because you need to know exactly who you are dealing with at each stage of the process and when negotiating settlement for each claim.

Insurance Settlement Secret # 8

The success or failure of your <u>Vehicle Damages</u> and <u>Medical Payments claims</u> will have a **direct impact** on the success or failure of your <u>Liability Injury claim</u> against the at-fault driver.

In order to successfully claim for Vehicle Damages and Medical Payments, you need to be familiar with exactly what Insurance Coverage you have.

The key source to learn this is from your own **Automobile Insurance Policy.**

Your Automobile Insurance Policy

A lot of people are intimidated by contracts and legal documents. Anything to do with Insurance Companies, Lawyers or Doctors can seem very complex to ordinary people who are not dealing with these issues every day.

Most people purchase Insurance and stuff the Automobile Policy in a drawer and rarely if ever look at it again.

People pay for Insurance for the one thing it can bring, peace of mind. If there is a problem, let the Insurance Company worry about it.

This is true, but it is important that when you have to make any type of claim, which inevitably at some point most of us will, you need to know what is going on to protect yourself.

The **key source** of that information is your **Automobile Policy.**

If you know how to read the Policy you are very well armed to protect yourself and your rights when making different types of claims.

The Automobile Policy is a **CONTRACT** between **YOU**, the Insured driver, and **your Insurance Company.**

Any claims made by an Insured driver against his or her Insurance Company will be according to the terms written down in the Automobile Insurance Policy.

If you need to find out information about exactly what your Insurance Company will pay then all you need to do is read your Policy.

If you cannot find your copy. Request a copy from your Insurer. They will be happy to send you a copy because you are their customer.

What does an Automobile Policy contain?

Liability Coverage

Liability Coverage is considered the most important type of car insurance, and it's required by most state automobile insurance laws.

This type of car insurance protects you against the cost of damage and injury that you cause to another in an automobile accident.

It is actually made up of two different policies, **bodily injury liability, and property damage liability.**

Bodily injury insurance pays for injuries caused to other individuals in the event of a motor vehicle accident.

Property (Vehicle) damage liability insurance pays for any damage caused to other vehicles in the event of a motor vehicle accident.

Automobile policies usually include three numbers (e.g. 25/50/15).

These numbers refer to automobile liability insurance and are often referred to as the split limits of liability insurance.

This means that in our example your coverage includes protection up to:

- $25,000 worth of bodily injury caused to another person
- $50,000 total for bodily injuries caused to everyone per accident
- $15,000 worth of property damage.

Each state's car insurance laws will require a certain level of automobile liability insurance.

Insurance Settlement Tip # 5

See the Mini Guide to State Legislation & Liability Limits at the end of this book.

The at-fault driver may have only the <u>minimum liability</u> limits required in your state, or he or she may have <u>purchased extra protection</u>.

The only way for your to know this is to <u>request the liability limits</u> from the At Fault Insurance Company when you open a claim with them.

Insurance Settlement Tip # 6

See the Sample letter at the end of this book for <u>Opening a Liability claim</u>.

Medical Payments and PIP Coverage

This coverage provides for the immediate treatment of injuries caused by a car accident. You, your family members and other passengers in your vehicle are included in the coverage, regardless of who is at fault for the accident.

Medical payments coverage may also compensate for lost wages or services of a person injured in the motor vehicle accident. You will need to refer to the specifics of your policy.

Personal Injury Protection (PIP)

Many PIP or Personal Injury Protection policies provide compensation for lost wages, funeral expenses, and pain and suffering. PIP is similar to medical payments coverage, but is usually more extensive.

Most states that require personals injury protection are *"no fault"* states, but Maryland, Delaware, and Oregon also provide this protection.

Collision Coverage

Collision coverage is for damage to the Insured Vehicle as a result of a motor vehicle accident, no matter who caused the accident. Collision coverage usually requires the payment of a **deductible** when a claim is made.

Under-Insured Motorist (UM) Coverage

Under-insured motorist coverage pays for the <u>cost of your injuries</u> that <u>exceed</u> the <u>other driver's maximum limits</u>.

Uninsured Motorist (UIM) Coverage

Uninsured motorist insurance protects you in the situation where the <u>other driver</u> has <u>no liability coverage</u>.

Under-insured and Uninsured Motorist coverage are not usually required in most states, but some states require one or the other, and a few even require both. They are frequently required in *"no fault"* states.

Generally, insurance companies will only allow purchase of Under-insured and Uninsured motorist coverage up to the insured's current bodily injury limit.

Automobile Policy Sections

Your Automobile Policy will have different sections which contain the exact information on what Insurance Coverage you have for each of these type of claims.

Sections are usually designated by letters A,B,C and D etc.

Therefore a Typical Automobile Policy will breakdown your Insurance Coverage by order of importance.

<u>Liability</u> is the most serious therefore it in usually falls under the first section, e.g. *"Section A"*.

Next in importance would be <u>Medical Payments</u> so it may fall under Section B.

In No Fault States the <u>Personal Injury Protection (PIP)</u> coverage may fall under one combined section.

Collision coverage is for damage to the Insured Vehicle as a result of a motor vehicle accident and usually would fall under Section C.

Sections D and E may cover Uninsured and Unidentified Motor Vehicle coverage.

However, you will need to **read** your own Automobile Insurance Policy for the exact designations.

There will also usually be sections at the back of the policy with General Provisions, Definitions, and Exclusions and also a section for Statutory Conditions.

Under each Section heading will usually be a paragraph stating exactly what benefits you will receive if you are involved in an accident.
Usually the Section of Liability coverage will begin with the words:

> *"The Insurer shall agree to **indemnify** the Insured for......."*

or

> *"The Insurer shall agree to **pay** the Insured for......."*

The most important word in Insurance is *"Indemnify"*. This word indemnify is the underlying principle in all Insurance contracts.

Under the Principle of Indemnity the Insured will not recover more than the value of the loss. To indemnify is to place someone back in the same financial position that they were in immediately prior to the loss.

The principle of indemnity provides that insureds are to collect the amount of their financial loss, no more and no less, subject to such other provisions of the policy as deductible and limits.

Below this paragraph will be subsections, usually with numbers, which list more benefits, but also conditions, warranties and representations.

Conditions

Conditions are stated on the Policy and impose on you the Insured requirements to do or not to do something.

Examples of conditions are limitation periods for making your claim, time periods for paying a loss, subrogation, assignment and cancelation.

Subrogation

Most people outside the Insurance world will be unfamiliar with the word *"subrogation"*. It is really important for the Insurance adjusters.

"Subrogation" means that if the Insurance Company has paid you for a loss, such as for repairs to your vehicle, as a result of an accident caused by another driver, then the Insurance Company has the right to seek "subrogation" (i.e. payment) from the at-fault Insurance Company.

Later in this book, you will learn how *"subrogation"* of your vehicle damages by your Insurance Company will help you in your Liability claim against the at fault driver's Insurance Company.

Warranties

A warranty is the promise or statement made by the insured that a specified state of affairs will be maintained for the duration of the contract term. An example of a warranty would be that you, the insured, promise to maintain your vehicle to road safety standards.

Representations

Representations are statements made by you, the insured driver, to your insurance company before the contract is made.

The Insurance Company salesperson or broker will calculate your premium based on the representations you have made.

Examples of representations are advising the Insurance Company that you will be using the vehicle to commute to work, or that someone else also will be driving your vehicle.

Failure to disclose important details like these could be treated as nondisclosure or misrepresentation.

If you have misrepresented the facts to your insurance company, you may lose the right to recover for your claim.

The key point is that the Automobile Policy is a contract with **obligations for you**, the insured driver, and the **Insurance Company.**

In order for each side to uphold their side of the contract there must be utmost good faith on both sides.

There is an exception to this where the Insurance Company elects to overlook the misrepresentation by you, the Insured. This is called a *"Waiver"*.

This means the Insurance Company has decided not to enforce the right to deny coverage even though you were in breach of a condition.

However, the general rule is that you should always give full disclosure and never make misrepresentations to your Insurance Company.

Insurance Settlement Secret # 9

When you speak with you Insurance Company Claims Adjuster, if you can refer to the Section in your policy by name, for example *"Section B, Medical Payments"*, and know your way around the policy, the adjuster will take you very seriously.

This is because the adjusters themselves constantly refer to the policy if they have questions on coverage.

If you understand the contents of your automobile policy and what coverage is available for each type of claim, then this will help you when you are negotiating settlement.

The *"At Fault"* Driver's Automobile Policy

Another reason to be familiar with the contents of your Automobile policy, is in relation to your Liability claim against the at-fault driver.

If you are injured in an automobile accident caused by another driver, then you will be making a Liability claim against that driver's Insurance Company.

The at-fault driver will also have an Automobile Policy with his or her Insurance Company.

It is very unlikely that the at-fault driver's Insurance Company would ever release to you the claimant a copy of the policy. In fact they may be prohibited by privacy laws.

However, the at-fault driver's Policy should have a section for Liability which would be very similar in content, if not identical, to the same section in your policy.

Insurance Settlement Secret # 10

Therefore, if you wish to get a good idea of the at-fault driver's Insurance Company obligations to you for your injuries as a result of an accident, just read your own policy section on Liability.

In the Liability section you can read how the insurance company *"agrees to indemnify"* the insured driver, (or someone who has consent to drive the vehicle), for any *"liability"* for loss or damage arising from the use or operation of the automobile which results in "BODILY INJURY" or "DEATH" to any person or "DAMAGE TO PROPERTY".

Therefore, since you know that the other driver is at fault, he or she is obliged by law to recompense you, i.e. pay you for your loss and pain and suffering. This can amount to tens of thousands of dollars to several million dollars.

Technically, your **cause of action** is still against the **at-fault driver.**

However, the at-fault driver, because of this clause in his or her insurance policy, doesn't have to worry about paying you because the Insurance Company *"agrees to indemnify"* him or her for any bodily injury or loss he or she causes to you.

Very Important!

The at-fault driver has a **Contract** with his or her Insurance Company to Indemnify for the loss he or she has to pay to you.

The at-fault driver and his Insurance Company each have signed the contract and have obligations under the contract.

You, as an innocent injured party are not part of that contract. You didn't agree to its contents or sign it. You were not part of it and do not have "PRIVITY" of contract. Therefore you cannot enforce their contract.

However, the at-fault driver's Insurance Company knows that if the facts show that their driver caused the accident, at any time up to the Statute of Limitation expiration date, you can start a legal action against their driver.

If and when you do that, the at-fault driver's Insurance Company is **bound by the contract to pay** for their driver's legal and defense costs, including paying settlement to you.

In other words, the at-fault driver's Insurance Company knows that **eventually they will have to pay**. They cannot get out of this once liability is established showing their driver caused the accident where you or your passenger were injured.

Insurance Settlement Secrets # 11

In order to avoid all these extra legal costs to defend against any action you start against their Insured, the At Fault driver's company would much rather deal directly with you.

By legal costs, I mean not just costs for a lawyer you might hire but also costs for defense lawyers that the Insurance Company would hire.

In reality and practice this happens for many injuries. The at-fault driver's Insurance Company pays you directly, instead of waiting for their driver to pay you and then *"indemnifying"* (reimbursing) their driver.

Why I am going into such detail on this point?

I am only doing this to show you that, just as you had Liability coverage for Bodily Injury and property damage if you caused a collision with another vehicle, so the at-fault driver, most of the time will have coverage for loss or injury to you up to certain limits.

What if the at-fault driver has no coverage?

Usually the only way for an at-fault driver to have no Liability coverage is if he or she actually has no automobile insurance.

In most states and provinces the absolute minimum coverage is for Liability to other drivers, passengers and pedestrians.

If the at-fault driver has no valid insurance, either because he or she could not renew their policy or it was canceled, then you still need to be able to get paid for your injury and loss.

The only other place you can go to is your own Insurance Company.

Can you claim from your own Insurance Company for the your injury and loss caused by an uninsured driver?

Insurance Settlement Secret # 12

If you have the coverage, yes you can. Look for the Section in your policy that covers "UNINSURED AUTOMOBILE AND UNIDENTIFIED AUTOMOBILE".

In our example this was in the Section D of the policy. Typically this Uninsured Automobile Coverage would come near the end of the policy .

The Key is to Know your Policy

Familiarize yourself with your Insurance Policy Coverage. Then you can confidently open the appropriate claims against the appropriate parties.

Therefore, if you have Collision coverage, you can open a claim for vehicle damages with your own Insurer.

If you live in a No-Fault State and have Personal Injury Protection Coverage (PIP) you can open a claim with your own Insurance Company.

Locate and have a quick read of your own Automobile Insurance Policy.

Once you understand what is covered under your Insurance Policy, you are ready to open your different claims.

How to Open a Vehicle Damages Claim

Step 1: Notify Your Insurance Company of the Motor Vehicle Accident

After an accident you should call your own Insurance Company to let them know that you have been in an accident. This is usually a requirement of your Automobile Policy.

When you call your Insurance Company and tell them you have been in an accident, they will connect you to their Claims Department.

By calling your own Insurance Company, you are giving them "Notice" of the Motor Vehicle Accident and your claims.

Insurance Settlement Secret # 13

You MUST <u>open a claim for vehicle damages</u> even though there is only a *"slight scratch"* off the paint. It will be very important for the success of your Liability Injury Claim against the at-fault driver's Insurance Company.

Opening a Claim for vehicle damages, whether through your own Insurance company, or the at-fault driver's Insurance Company will help establish the **first element of your Injury claim** -That the other driver or drivers were at fault and CAUSED the motor vehicle accident.

Therefore, even though there is *only a scratch* to your vehicle, you should definitely open a vehicle damages claim.

Should you open a Vehicle/Property Damages claim with your own Insurance Company or with the at-fault driver's Insurance company?

Opening a Vehicle Damages Claim with Your Own Insurance Company

If you open a Property/Vehicle Damages claim through your own Insurance Company under **Collision coverage**, settlement is usually much faster than claiming against the other driver's Insurance Company.

However, your Collision coverage may have limits, so any excess damages will have to be claimed against the At-Fault driver's Insurance Company under you Liability claim.

Insurance Settlement Secret # 14

In most Insurance Companies the Claims department will have different *specialists* to deal with each type of claim.

Therefore, if you are opening a Property/Vehicle Damages claim with your own Insurance Company, then you will be speaking with an adjuster who specializes in property and vehicle damages only.

Your Property Damage Adjuster will ask you questions about the motor vehicle accident over the phone. If there are serious or unusual circumstances they may wish to send out a Field Adjuster to meet with you for a **statement**.

Insurance Settlement Secret # 15

When you are making any type of claim against your own Insurance Company, you must remember that you are their <u>client</u> and customer.

Therefore, the relationship is <u>not</u> supposed to be <u>adversarial</u> in any way. They are there to serve you according to the contract terms of your Policy.

Therefore, it is to **your advantage** to cooperate with your own Insurance Company.

This is the difference between making claims with your own Insurance Company instead of making a Third Party Liability Claim against the at -fault driver's Insurance Company.

When you make a <u>Liability Claim</u> against the <u>at -fault driver's Insurance Company</u>, the relationship <u>is adversarial</u> and you have to be more careful in volunteering information.

(See section on <u>How to Open an Liability Claim</u>.)

Insurance Settlement Secret # 16

However, even though you are not in an adversarial relationship with your own Insurance Company you should not give much detail about your injury to your Property Damages Claims adjuster, as he or she is not trained to deal with injuries.

Simply state when asked that *"Yes"* you are injured and you *"are getting medical attention"*. The Property Claims adjuster does not need to know more than this.

If you have <u>Collision Coverage</u> under your Automobile Policy you will be able to open a claim for damages to your vehicle.

Collision Coverage

Collision coverage pays (*"indemnifies"* you) for damage to your vehicle caused by a collision with another object or upset. This includes your vehicle striking or being struck by another automobile, as well as single vehicle accidents.

Usually a Property Damage Adjuster will send out an *Appraiser* to appraise the damages of your vehicle to see how much it will cost to repair.

If you can drive your vehicle you may be asked to take it to an *Inspection Station*.

Your Insurance company will usually require that your vehicle be repaired at one of their *"Preferred"* shops.

Your Insurance Company will cover the **cost of repairs** or pay you for the **Actual Cash Value (ACV)** of your vehicle if it is a total loss.

If you were not at fault for the accident you will have to sign a document granting ***"Right of Subrogation"*** to your Insurance Company so they can get back the amount they paid you from the at-fault driver's Insurance Company.

Deductible

There may also be a *Deductible*. A deductible is a certain dollar amount, usually $250 - $1000 which can be deducted from any property damages paid to you.

Insurance Settlement Secret # 17

Often the Insurance Company will *waive the deductible* and pay you the full amount of your damages especially if you are not at fault for the accident.

They will likely only do this if you ask nicely and do not have a history accident claims. If you are a good customer your Insurance

42

Company may want to keep on good terms with you.

However, this is if you were not responsible for the accident. Also it is still a matter of the Property Adjuster's discretion.

A typical **Property / Vehicle Damage settlement** includes:

1. The Towing costs
2. Storage costs
3. Car rental
4 Repair costs or ACV (Actual Cash Value) amount for vehicles that are declared a Total Loss.

What if you have **no Collision Coverage** on your automobile Insurance Policy or *your deductible is higher than the damage*?

If you have no Collision Coverage with your Insurance Company, then you have the *choice* of paying for your own vehicle damages and/or claim vehicle damages from the At-Fault driver's Insurance Company.

Insurance Settlement Secret # 18

If you have no collision coverage and are confident you did not cause the accident, open a claim for vehicle damages against the At -Fault driver's Insurance Company.

They will call you once they hear about the accident either from their driver or from your Insurance Company after you reported the accident.

The At -Fault driver's Insurance Company will want to investigate who was at-fault for the accident before they will make any payment for your vehicle damages.

However, Insurance Companies are becoming much more efficient at determining who is at fault.

The At-Fault driver's Insurance Company Property Damage adjuster may simply make some phone calls to verify the facts with their own Insured driver. If fault is clear then your Claim for vehicle damages will be processed quickly in days or weeks

If there are doubts on liability, he or she may send out an *"Independent Adjuster"* to meet with your for a statement.

(See the Liability section on determining who is at fault.)

Once the At-fault Driver's Insurance Company is clear that their driver was **"at fault"** for the accident they will send an appraiser to assess the damages to your vehicle.

Then they will issue a check for your damages. You will be asked to sign a Final Release for Property Damages only. Then you will receive your check.

The Property/ Vehicle damages claim is the first and easiest to settle. Injury claims usually take much longer to sort out.

Insurance Settlement Secret # 19

If because of necessity, or because your deductible was greater than the damage, you paid for your own vehicle damages, you should still OPEN a Property Damages claim with the at-fault driver's Insurance Company and have them reimburse you for what you paid.

As with your own Insurance Company, the At-Fault driver's Insurance Company will have specialists who deal with Property Damages only.

Insurance Settlement Tip # 7

However, sometimes the At Fault driver's Insurance Company will have their Bodily Injury Adjuster, who will handle your injury claim, also take care of your vehicle damages claim.

Insurance Settlement Secret # 20

Often the At-Fault Insurance Company Adjuster will **try to settle your injury claim** at the ***same time*** as your **Vehicle Damages claim.**

E.g. You have $1,500 vehicle damages. The at-fault driver's Insurance Company may offer you another $1,500 on top for your injury claim.

You may think this is great. Now they're giving you a nice check for $3,000.

Insurance Settlement Secret # 21

Most Insurance Companies are willing to pay $2,500 for the injury alone, and that's without even a medical report! Therefore, if you accept this you are getting a minimum of $1,000 less than you could.

(More on this later in the <u>Negotiating Your Settlement</u> section).

Rule of thumb: *do not settle your injury claim* at the same time you settle Vehicle/Property damage claim.

Settle each claim separately. This will guarantee you do not get *"shortchanged"* on your injury settlement.

How to Open a Medical Payments Claim

If you are injured in an accident you do not have time to wait for settlement from the at-fault driver's Insurance Company, which could take months or years. You need medical help immediately, and that means you will have medical expenses.

When you call your own Insurance Company and notify them that you were in an accident, the Claims Adjuster will usually ask you if your were injured.

If you are injured and you have Medical Payments Coverage (or PIP coverage in No-Fault states) they will set up a Claim for you at the same time as a Property/Vehicle damage claim.

Then an Medical Payments Adjuster will be in contact with you to monitor and pay for your treatments and benefits. Very often the person handling this type of claim will have some form of clinical background in Physiotherapy or Kinesiology.

The Medical Payments claim is to cover your medical treatment costs and a portion of loss of wages from time off due to the Motor Vehicle Accident.

Your Medical Payments Claim is through **your own Insurance Company**. Under your **Automobile Policy**.

Medical Payments will usually only be paid if you do not have any other *"Primary"* Insurance coverage such as Private Short Term or Long Term Disability coverage, either on your own or through your Employer.

If you do have Private Health Insurance Coverage or other Health Insurance then you will first have to open a claim with them to cover your medical expenses.

Private Health Insurance policies usually cover only up to a certain limit, such as 80%. The shortfall you can then claim against your own Insurer under Medical Payments or PIP in No Fault states.

This principle applies to coverage for <u>Income Loss</u> as well as <u>Medical expenses</u>.

Medical Payments claims operate on a *"no fault"* basis. This is why you make your claim against your own Insurance Company no matter who is at fault for the accident.

This also means that your relationship with your Medical Payments Adjuster should not be adversarial. This is a customer client relationship.

The Medical Payments Adjusters typically are very caring and hard working and they are there to help you. They will monitor your treatments, pay the treatment clinics and pay a percentage of lost wages.

The only point of contention is when it comes to winding up treatment. Some claimants may disagree about whether they have made a recovery or not. Then it comes down to the opinions of **your family doctor** against those of an **Independent Medical Examiner**.

Consult with your Insurance Company Medical Payments Adjuster for more exact details.

Medical Payments and PIP coverage can be quite extensive and treatments for injuries can last several years. The length of your recovery period will be a significant factor in any Liability claim you have against the at-fault driver's Insurance Company.

Insurance Settlement Secrets # 22

If your own Insurance Company will not cover the shortfall, then these left over expenses and costs can be added to your Liability Injury Claim against the at-fault Driver's Insurance Company.

What to do if you have no Health Coverage?

Unfortunately there are many people who do not have any Health Coverage. It could be that after an accident you find you have no coverage at all through private insurance or through your own Insurance Policy, to cover medical expenses.

Insurance Settlement Secrets # 23

In the case where you have no Private Health Insurance, Employer Health Insurance and no coverage under your policy for your basic medical expenses after a motor vehicle accident, there is another option of last resort.

You have the option of requesting that the at-fault driver's Insurer cover your <u>medical treatment expenses.</u>

This is even though at the end of the treatment you will be seeking a full settlement for your injury from the <u>at-fault driver's Insurance Company</u>.

Insurance Settlement Tip # 8

See the **sample letter** at the end of the book you can use to request that the at-fault driver's Insurance Company cover your immediate medical expenses.

You may be asked to prove by a letter from your own Insurance Company confirming that you have no Medical Payments coverage, before the At- Fault Driver's Insurance Company would consider paying your medical expenses.

By sending this letter you are showing you are trying to *"mitigate"* your loss. Literally this means you are trying to control or limit your losses by getting better.

If liability is established showing you were injured and their driver was at fault then the at-fault driver's Insurance Company has an **obligation** to pay for your medical expenses if you can show you have no other way to pay for your treatments.

Remember, if it wasn't for the motor vehicle accident you would not have been injured. Therefore, all the **consequences flowing from your accident**, including medical treatment expenses are foreseeable and the at-fault driver's Insurance Company knows eventually it will have to pay.

The at-fault driver's Insurance Company also knows that if they don't help you when you have no other way of getting treatment, that your condition may get worse and they could have a much larger settlement exposure.

Note: Any money that is paid by the At-Fault Insurance Company to cover treatment **cannot** be added to your settlement demand at the negotiation stage when you make your demand for *"pain and suffering"*.

See <u>Paying For Medical Treatment</u> section for more on this topic.

Liability

Who is "At Fault" for the Accident?

Insurance Settlement Secret # 24

Liability is a very big issue for the Insurance Companies. Whoever is **at fault** for the accident is **liable for the consequences** of the accident.

Determining who is at-fault or caused the accident may not be your priority when you are injured in an accident, but it is the **number one priority** for the Insurance Companies and their Adjusters who are handling the claims.

What does it mean to be *"At Fault"* for the accident? How do you know who is at fault?

You are *"at fault"* for the accident if you **CAUSED** the accident. If you caused the accident then your Insurance Company will be liable to pay for any injuries to others and their vehicle damages.

If the other driver was the cause of the accident then his or her Insurance Company will be liable to pay for any injuries to you or damages to your vehicle.

The Investigation Begins

When you open claims with your Insurance Company or the other driver's Insurance Company, they will investigate and establish who is at fault very early.

It is to your advantage to know in advance before making any claims against other Insurance Companies, to be certain who was at fault.

Liability: Who is at Fault?

The assumption is that you will **not** bring an injury claim against the other driver's insurance company <u>if you were the cause</u> of the accident.

In most cases it will be clear who was at-fault and the **at-fault driver's Insurance Company** will contact you concerning your injury.

If it is not clear, e.g. both you and the other party were each responsible, you may still claim against the other driver's insurance company and any claim you have will usually be reduced by your percentage of fault.

You will know soon after the accident who is held at-fault because if you disclose all the facts, which you must do with your <u>own</u> Insurance Company, and you were the cause of the accident, then your own Insurance Company will tell you that you are at fault.

Your own Insurance Company will probably reserve judgment on who was at fault until they have all the facts.

If your own Insurance Company tells you that you were at fault for the accident, it almost always means you are at fault.

How do you determine who is at fault for the accident?

In most motor vehicle accidents, once all the facts have been gathered, it is pretty clear who is at fault for the accident.

This is why the Insurance Companies from both sides, as soon as they are notified by their insured, will immediately investigate the facts surrounding the accident.

Insurance Settlement Secret # 25

This is a big deal for both your Insurance Company and the other driver's Insurance company. But it is **not a big deal for you if you were not at fault**.

Why? Because you were there. **You already know what happened**.

You already know the facts.

If you were clearly not at fault for the accident, then all you have to do is **describe the facts** as you saw and experienced them to the Police Officer, if he comes to the scene and asks you questions.

When you call your Insurance Company, just tell them you were in an accident and repeat how the accident happened.

Your own Insurance Company Adjuster will ask you over the telephone for details and the circumstances of how the accident happened and he or she will enter your description of events on a computer.

If the facts are straightforward and fall into the **typical accident scenarios**, your Insurance Company Vehicle Damage Adjuster will likely advise you right there on the phone whether or not you were responsible.

Now is the time for complete honesty. Firstly, you must be 100% honest with yourself about what happened, and also honest with what you tell other people.

Why is honesty so important?

Insurance Settlement Secret # 26

Honesty is so important because, you can be sure that both your Insurance Company and the other driver's Insurance Company will send out adjusters to investigate every detail.

They will take photos, get police reports, talk to witnesses, and compare damages to the vehicles. They may get written statements from other drivers and from passengers.

If there is any question surrounding the facts, both Insurance Companies will send out professional independent adjusters whose sole purpose in life is to dig for facts and get to the cause of the accident as soon as possible

If something is not right or not clear, you can be sure that it will be noticed. If you have given false or contradictory information you can be sure you will be found out.

Insurance Settlement Secret # 27

If you were hiding something or were not honest you will be exposed and your own Insurance Company will not be happy with you. They may increase your premiums or worse cancel your policy.

Special note to the Reader

I am certain that someone who has bought this book is not in any way the type of person who would not be honest!

However, we are all human, especially when it comes to driving. There is a lot of pride at stake, as well as money, increase of premiums and driving record.

Sadly, there are quite a few people out there who will try to twist the facts to avoid being held at fault.

Common examples of dishonesty:

Little White Lies

1. Saying you had put on your signal when you did not.
2. Saying you had a green or amber light when it was red.
3. Saying your speed was much slower than it was.
4. Saying you were wearing your seat belt when you were not.

Insurance Settlement Tip # 9

There are easy ways to tell if you were really wearing your seat-belt:

1. You may have a cut or injury on your face from hitting the windshield or the windshield itself may have been smashed by your head.

2. It is very common for a passenger to mention in his or her statement that you were not wearing the seat belt.

3. Investigators can often tell from examining the seat belt whether it was worn or functioning properly.

Big Lies

1. Telling the other driver you have no Insurance and that he or she will have to go to their own Insurance Company. Some people will even tell a police officer this.

(I have seen this tried on a number of occasions. Eventually the Insurance adjuster tracks down, through their license or plate #, the details of a valid Insurance Policy.)

Honesty

I emphasize HONESTY because there is so much at stake for you and the Insurance Companies. With so many professional adjusters, investigators, doctors and lawyers looking at the circumstances surrounding your claim, EVENTUALLY all will be REVEALED.

Many accident victims believe they should **not cooperate** with Insurance Company Adjusters for statements and hold back giving details, especially revealing information that demonstrates any fault on their part.

In my years of experience, this is the **wrong** approach because it only drags out the whole process.

In the long run it does not benefit you to hold back the true facts.

Eventually the facts will come out. It is much better for you to be **truthful and honest** with yourself and everyone else **right from the start** so that your claim cannot later down the road be picked apart by Defense Counsel for the Insurance Companies.

If you were partly at fault then it is much better to explain this right at the start to your own Insurance Company, usually the Property Damage Adjuster if you have Collision coverage.

If you are partly at fault but not the main cause of the motor vehicle accident then you can still proceed with your injury claim against the other driver's insurance company, and the value of your settlement will likely be reduced by your percentage of fault.

The key is that your injury claim must be based on 100% HONESTY otherwise your claim will eventually fall apart.

Don't worry, there is plenty of settlement money available even for minor injury claims.

I will show you exactly how to calculate the value of your claim just like the PROS so that you and you alone get maximum dollars for you injury claim.

Doing Your Own Investigation?

Many people are under the impression that they must do their own investigation, including taking scene photos, vehicle damage photos, and tracking down witnesses etc.

First of all, how can you expect to do this when you are injured and may be off work and in bed for days or weeks after the accident? You have enough on your mind without having to do an investigation!

Insurance Settlement Secret # 28

You DO NOT have to conduct your own investigation of the motor vehicle accident.

Why? Because you can get both Insurance Companies to do the investigating for you.

As I stated, both **your Automobile Insurance Company** and the **other driver's Insurance Company** will thoroughly investigate the accident.

All you have to do is **open a claim for Vehicle Damages** with your own Insurance Company if you have Collision coverage, or with the at fault driver's Insurance Company if you do not.

Neither Insurance Company wants to pay so they will investigate the accident thoroughly to get out of paying for your vehicle damages, including taking photos and making reports.

If the other driver is at fault, his or her Insurance Company will soon know this. How will they know?

Insurance Settlement Secret # 29

The Insurance Company that <u>ultimately pays</u> for your vehicle damages has <u>accepted</u> that their driver is at fault.

If there were any damages to your vehicle and you have <u>Collision</u> coverage under your policy, your Insurance Company will pay your damages right away without regard to fault.

But, if their investigation shows that the other driver was at fault for the accident, your Insurance Company will **seek reimbursement** for what they have paid you from their driver's Insurance Company. This is called *"Subrogation"*.

Once the at-fault driver's Insurance Company completes their investigation and sees their driver was at fault, they will pay your Insurance Company for the amount for the repairs to your vehicle.

Insurance Settlement Tip # 10

If you received payment from your own Insurance Company under your **Collision coverage** for your vehicle damages, call your Adjuster about 30 -45 days after the accident and verify if they have received subrogation, i.e. if they have been paid back what they paid you.

56

If your Insurance Company was paid back the amount they paid you for your vehicle damages, then you ABSOLUTELY KNOW that the other driver's Insurance Company has ACCEPTED that their driver is at-fault.

If their driver was only 50% at fault then they will only have paid back your Insurance Company 50% of the vehicle damages.

What if you had no collision coverage under your auto policy?

If you had no collision coverage under your auto policy, you will have opened a Property Damages claim against the at-fault driver's Insurance Company.

(See How to Open a Liability Claim, and also the Insurance Settlement Secrets Checklist at the end of this book.)

Obviously, the other driver's Insurance Company will not pay for your vehicle damages if their driver was not at fault.

But once their investigation confirms their driver was at fault, they must and will pay for your vehicle damages.

Once the other driver's Insurance Company has paid for your vehicle damages YOU KNOW and THEY KNOW that they have accepted that their driver was at fault.

This is why it is so important for you to open a Vehicle Damages claim, even if there is "only a scratch", either against your own Insurance Company if you have Collision coverage, or against the at-fault driver's Insurance Company.

Note: Some will argue that just because an Insurance Company has paid for your vehicle damages, doesn't mean they will accept liability for your injury under *"Tort"*. This is legalese and hot air.

Insurance Companies are not charities. Any Insurance Company that has paid for the vehicle damages of another driver's vehicle, has ACCEPTED that their driver is at fault, either completely or to a certain degree of fault.

Once the At-Fault Driver's Insurance company has accepted liability you have **established the first element of your injury claim** and the **Insurance Companies have done <u>all the investigation work</u>**!

The At-Fault Driver's Insurance Company now knows they have **liability exposure** for your injuries as a result of the motor vehicle accident.

You are well on your way to making your injury claim **"Bullet proof"**.

Motor Vehicle Accident in Another State

Where the Motor Vehicle Accident happened in another state the general rule is that the law of the state where the accident happened applies.

This would rarely make a difference for the rules of the road, as they are pretty standard.

However, where you are partially at fault this may make a difference in the outcome of your injury claim as states have different laws for determining comparative negligence, i.e. percentage of fault.

This will only be an issue when you are calculating the value of your injury claim. Obviously, if you are 50% at-fault for the accident you should consider this when making your settlement demand.

See section <u>How to Calculate the Value of Your Injury Claim</u>.

If you are partly at fault and are unsure about the law concerning comparative fault contact the State Department of Insurance where the accident happened.

Common Types of Motor Vehicle Accidents

There are a number of automobile accident scenarios where it is **clear** **who is at fault**. These follow the general <u>rules of the road</u>.

Insurance Settlement Secret # 30

In fact, these types of accidents are so common that many Insurance Companies are signatories to **Chart Settlement Agreements** between Insurance Companies.

Therefore, if the accident happened according to a particular scenario as illustrated in the Chart, then the Insurance company, for the driver who was *"at fault"* according to the chart, will pay.

This saves the Insurance Companies time and money haggling over who is responsible.

<u>Chart Settlement Agreements</u> set out a whole series of accident scenarios where fault is automatically determined by the position of the vehicles, traffic signs and type of location.

Insurance Settlement Secret # 31

These Chart Settlement Agreements are used to determine fault only for Vehicle Property Damages.

They are **not legally binding** and do not prevent a driver, who is found at fault for an accident by his or her own Insurance Company, from commencing or making a Liability Injury claim under Tort against the other driver's Insurance Company.

However, if you are found *"at fault"* under a Chart Agreement by your own Insurance Company for property damages, it is a good indicator that you will be liable to the other driver for their injuries, and vice versa.

On the next page is a guide to **common accident scenarios** according to the rules of the road for driving across North America to help you determine who was at fault for the accident.

There may be some exceptions according to your State or Municipality. For example: some jurisdictions do not allow a right turn on a red light.

Common Types of Motor Vehicle Accidents

1. Rear end Collisions:

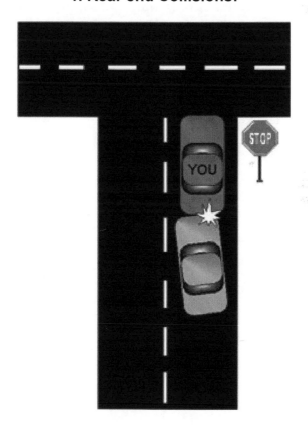

The general rule is if you are **rear ended by another vehicle** then 99% of the time the **other driver is 100 % at- fault.**

If you rear end another vehicle then you will very likely be held 100% at fault.

Exceptions for the General Rule for Rear end Collision may result in the lead vehicle being held to be partly if not entirely at fault for the accident.

The technical term for this is being *"contributarily negligent"*.

Examples of exceptions to the general rule for rear end collisions:

1. The lead vehicle is **turning into a driveway and doesn't put on a signal,** or the **signal light is not functioning** properly. Even if this is true the rear vehicle can still be held at least 50% at-fault.

2. The lead vehicle **stops abruptly** on the highway for **no good reason**. Example: They *"missed their exit"*, or they *"Didn't want to hit a rabbit"*.

This can cause a chain reaction and there the lead vehicle could be held 100% at fault. However, this exception is RARE and hard to prove.

3. The lead vehicle driver did a Traffic violation and was charged for dangerous maneuver, such an doing a U-turn on a highway or erratic driving while intoxicated.

As you can see, 99.9% of the time, if you are rear ended by another vehicle, that driver is AT-FAULT.

2. Left Turning Vehicle:

The general rule is that the vehicle making a left turn must wait until oncoming traffic has passed and it is safe to make the turn.

An exception to this general rule:

1. The oncoming vehicle was speeding and its speed was the partial or real cause of the accident. The driver would have to be charged and convicted of speeding to be held at fault.

Therefore, if he or she was not charged with speeding, even though a witness saw them going fast, the other driver's Insurance Company would find it hard to prove in court.

The bottom line is Left turning vehicles are supposed to yield to oncoming traffic. If they don't and the vehicles collide, the left turning vehicle will <u>almost always be found 100% at fault</u>.

3. Failure to Obey a Stop Sign or Failure to Yield.

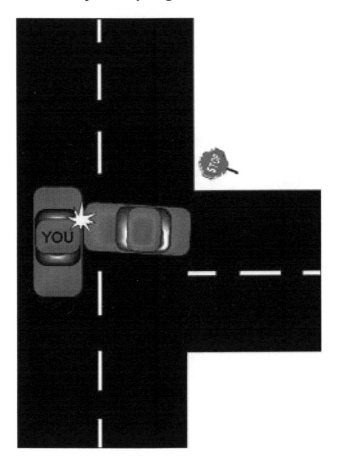

A driver who fails to obey a stop sign or leaves a stop or yield sign without yielding is 100% liable. This is also known as *"Failure to yield"* or *"Leaving the safety of a stop sign"*.

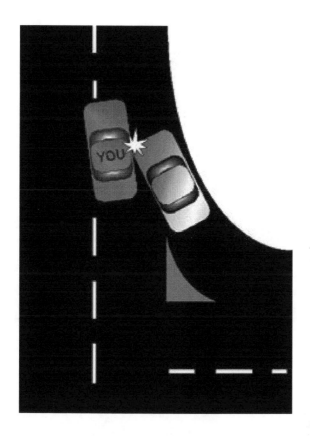

Within an intersection or while <u>exiting a lane way or driveway,</u> even though **no stop sign exits**, a **yield the right of way sign is deemed to exist**.

A driver who fails to obey a **<u>red traffic light</u>** is 100% responsible.

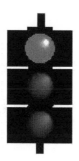

4. "4-Way" Stops and "T" Intersections.

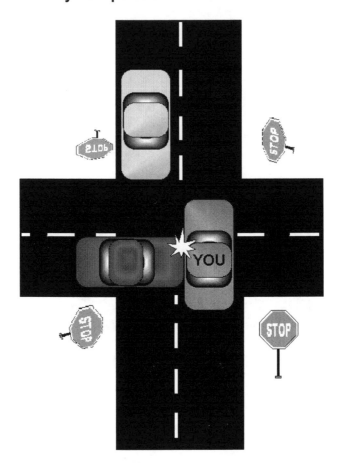

A "T" intersection where there are three stops signs or at a "4 Way" intersection with 4 stop signs, the vehicle reaching and stopping first at the intersection has the **right of way.** If another driver enters after you have the right of way and **collides with your vehicle** they are 100% at fault.

5. Failure to obey a Police Officer's Signal.

The driver of a vehicle <u>failing to obey a police officer's</u> signal, proceeding the <u>wrong way</u>, backing up, <u>making a U-turn</u> or <u>striking a parked vehicle</u>, is in each case 100% liable.

Liability is apportioned as shown regardless of whether the point of impact is front, center or rear of either vehicle.

6. Split Liability Circumstances:

Where two separate rules apply and each giving an opposing conclusion for responsibility then liability is apportioned 50/50.

Unresolved disputes for lack of independent proof may be apportioned 50/50.

An example of split liability would be:

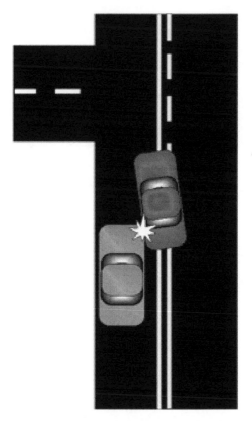

Where one vehicle is passing another vehicle in a no passing zone, while the other vehicle driver is driving while drunk, and both vehicles collide.

In this case both drivers would likely be held equally at fault.

Just because you are found 50% at fault is not a bar to making an injury claim against the other driver's insurance company. You can still proceed. However, any settlement will likely be reduced by your percentage of fault.

7. Pedestrians:

Where a pedestrian is struck by a vehicle the <u>driver of the vehicle</u> is almost always <u>100% at fault.</u>

However, there are exceptions even to this.

If a pedestrian is not looking where they are going and runs out into traffic, he or she can be found contributarily negligent.

This would reduce the driver's liability by the percentage by the degree of fault of the pedestrian for their own carelessness.

Insurance Settlement Secret # 32

In practice, even though a pedestrian was partly at fault, the Insurance Company will rarely push hard on this point because they know that if your case ever went to court they would get very little sympathy.

One rare exception where a pedestrian can be found 100% liable for his or her own injuries is where the pedestrian is attempting suicide or is lying in the middle of the road drunk at night on a highway.

E.g. I had a claim from a young man who was a pedestrian hit by our Insured vehicle at night on the highway. The young man had multiple fractures and was lucky to be alive.

The young man claimed that he had an epileptic seizure while trying to cross the highway late at night.

It seemed like our driver would be liable 100%. This was until we saw the Hospital Emergency Record which showed he was found 4 times over the legal limit for alcohol. The man was lying. His claim was denied because his own actions were the cause of his injuries.

8. Chain reactions.

Chart Settlement Agreements have special rules for apportioning vehicle property damages in chain reactions.

This is more for the convenience of Insurance Companies in settling these complex accidents.

There are several scenarios for chain reactions.

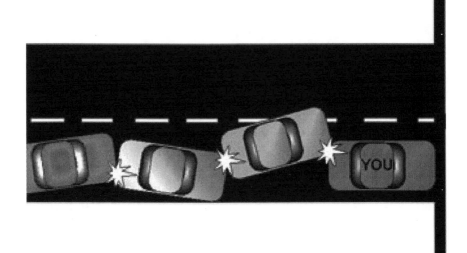

1. **You are the lead vehicle** and several cars **hit you from behind**, then unless you were charged with something like DWI or Traffic Violation for dangerous maneuver, you are absolutely **not** at fault.

2. Where there was an accident or **impact between two lead vehicles** and then other vehicles coming from behind cannot stop in time and hit the vehicle behind the lead vehicle, pushing it into the lead vehicle for a **second impact.**

In this case the **vehicle behind the lead vehicle could be found 50-100% at fault** for causing the accident.

Both lead vehicles could claim against the rear vehicles but the vehicle behind the lead vehicle that caused the first impact would have any settlement reduced by the amount of their responsibility.

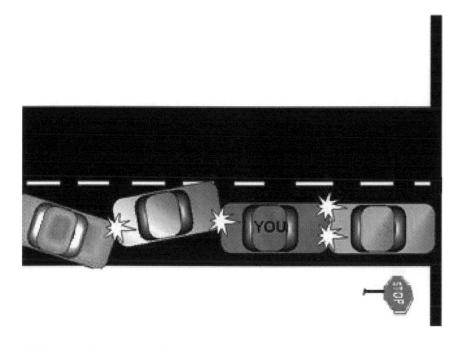

If You are just behind the lead vehicle, the KEY test is whether the driver of the <u>vehicle in front of you</u> felt **ONE IMPACT OR TWO IMPACTS.**

An exception to this may be where the other vehicles coming from behind should have easily been able to stop, but didn't. However, this is hard to prove.

3. The other basic type of chain reaction is where several cars are **stopped at an intersection with a traffic light or stop sign** and the **rear vehicle is going too fast** or is not paying attention and **hits the last vehicle and it is pushed forward into the other vehicles** and so on.

In this case the **rear vehicle** would be the **cause** of the accident.

You may be thinking, **who do you claim against** in a chain reaction with so many vehicles?

Insurance Settlement Secret # 33

If you were injured in a chain reaction accident and you were not the cause of the accident (or not the main cause), then you can make an injury claim against all and any of the Insurance Companies of the other vehicles behind you in chain reaction.

If you think the lead vehicle was the cause of the accident then you can also claim against that driver. This falls under the legal term of *"Joint and Several liability"* which simply means that where there is shared blame, each party can be held responsible to the Injured party for the whole amount.

In practice, where there is shared responsibility, the Insurance Companies can recover any settlement they make with you. All they have to do is pursue what they paid to you from the other Insurance Companies. It becomes their problem, not yours.

9. Commercial Parking Lots and Shopping Plazas

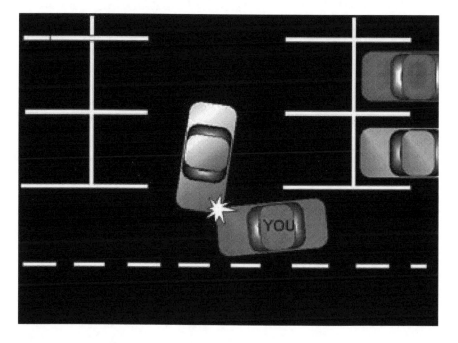

Any vehicle traveling on a portion of a public parking lot designated by the property owners or by its configuration as a *"thoroughfare"* or *"throughway"* shall have a right of way over vehicles entering it from a feeder lane.

10. Opening door of a vehicle and hitting another vehicle.

A driver is 100% liable if the open door of his vehicle causes damage to another vehicle.

11. Single Vehicle Accidents

A single vehicle accident is where there is no impact with another vehicle. The most common type of single vehicle accident is where a **vehicle loses control** and goes off the road. Sadly this often happens just after graduation with young people packed in a vehicle late at night.

Where you are a passenger in a vehicle driven by someone else and you are injured you can make a <u>claim for Medical Payments</u> against your own Automobile Insurance Company, if you have Insurance, and then you can also make a <u>Liability Injury Claim</u> against the Insurance Company that insures the driver of the vehicle.

Insurance Settlement Secret # 34

Sometimes the driver and you, the injured passenger, are Insured by the same Automobile Policy. You may be able to make a <u>Liability Claim</u> against your own Insurance Policy. This is called a **"PASSENGER HAZARD"** claim.

I have given you general overview of the common types of accidents and how to determine liability and who is at fault for these types of accidents.

If you have any doubts or questions a good source is the Property Damage Adjuster with your own Insurance Company who will call you about the damages to your vehicle.

He or she will be glad to tell you that the other Insurance Company is responsible for the accident. Likewise, if he or she feels you are responsible he or she will tell right away and your premium may be increased.

Most people, will be able to use *"common sense"* and know when the other party is responsible for the accident.

E.g. Common sense will tell you that it is not reasonable to be making a left turn in an intersection while at the same time filing your nails (as one young woman driver admitted doing).

How to Open a Liability Claim

Once you are clear that the other driver was responsible and liable for the accident then all you have to do is call your own Insurance Company and tell them what happened and give them the Contact and Insurance information that the other driver gave you when you exchanged information after the accident.

As soon as you notify your own Insurance Company, they will immediately be in contact with the other driver and his or her Insurance Company.

The first person who will contact you from the other driver's Insurance Company will likely be a **Property Damage Adjuster**.

Insurance Settlement Secret # 35

Some unscrupulous Insurance Company Adjusters may try to make you feel that you are at fault even when it was their driver who caused the accident.

They may try and intimidate you by suggesting you don't know anything about Insurance. They do this in the hope you will believe them or become frustrated and drop your claim.

But since you <u>know</u> that you were not at fault and that the other driver was the cause of the accident then you can be <u>calm and confident</u>.

When they ask you on the telephone what happened all you need to do is <u>confirm the facts</u>.

Most Insurance Company Injury Adjusters will be polite and courteous and will want to settle your claim promptly and fairly.

If the facts are similar to the scenarios as illustrated in the previous section, then it will be pretty clear who was at fault and the At-Fault Driver's Insurance Adjuster will not push the point.

Insurance Settlement Secret # 36

The At-Fault Insurance Company Adjusters almost never come out and say directly or in writing that their driver caused the accident or that they accept full liability.

It is a quirk of the profession, not to admit to anything in case later down the road the claim goes to court and something they said or wrote is held against them as evidence.

This does NOT mean that they are denying liability.

In practice, most injury claims are paid and settled without the At-Fault Insurance Company ever admitting that their driver was at fault.

Written Signed Statements

The modern trend is to avoid getting written signed statements where the facts fit clearly into accident scenarios where there is no question of who is at fault.

However, if there are complications such as passengers, multiple vehicles, fatalities and other factors, then statements will be sought by the At- Fault Insurance Company.

The At-Fault driver's Insurance Company may want to send an Adjuster to meet with you to obtain a written signed statement.

Usually the Insurance Adjuster will meet with you to ask you questions and he or she will write this all down. Then you will be asked to read the statement and if you agree with the facts, you will be asked to sign the statement.

How good a statement is depends on the ability and experience of the Insurance Adjuster asking the questions.

A statement will contain the basic facts as stated by you.

Insurance Settlement Secret # 37

The following are some elements that should be in the statement:

1. Your name
2. Age
3. Address
4. Time and date of the accident
5. Weather conditions
6. Traffic conditions
7. Posted speed limits
8. Actual driving speed
9. Whether you or your passengers were wearing seat belts
10. Whether you were stopped
11. If your were turning, did you put on your signal light?
12. Description of how the accident happened
13. What was your first reaction?
14. Were you able to get out of the vehicle immediately?
15. Whether you saw any vehicle damages
16. Did your speak with the other driver or drivers?
17. Were there any witnesses?
18. Were you injured in the motor vehicle accident?
19. Whether the police or ambulance came
20. Whether you went to the hospital
21. Depending how long after the accident the statement was taken, what is your present condition?

As you can see there is a lot of information here.

Insurance Settlement Secret # 38

Some auto accident claimants are against the idea of giving a signed statement of the facts to the At Fault Driver's Insurance Company.

The argument is that you may state something in the recorded statement that may be used against you later to deny your claim.

It is certainly true that your claim against the at-fault driver's Insurance Company puts you in an adversarial position and you have to be careful about what you say.

On the other hand, if you are **not at fault** for the accident and the other driver was at-fault because they *"rear-ended"* your vehicle, *"turned left in front of you"* or *"ran a red light"*, then the <u>sooner</u> the At-Fault Insurance Company <u>confirms</u> this the sooner they can process your claim and pay your settlement.

The bottom line is once it is clear from the facts that their driver was at-fault, the Insurance Company will treat you with utmost respect and will have to honor your claim.

As you read in the previous sections, most motor vehicle accidents fall under **common types of accident scenarios** and usually it is not difficult to ascertain who was at fault.

Therefore, if the At Fault Driver's Insurance Company is seeking a written statement from you it suggests they have some <u>doubts on liability.</u>

It is in your interests to <u>remove their doubts on liability</u> so that the At-Fault Insurance Company can process your injury claim.

If there are any remaining doubts on liability your injury claim will simply stall.

I would agree that it is best not to volunteer to give a signed statement.

However, where the accident does not fit in the typical scenarios or their are multiple vehicles such as for chain reactions, or multiple injuries or a fatality, then the fact that you don't want to give a statement may indicate you are <u>hiding something</u>.

Remember, if you have reviewed the most common types of motor vehicle accidents and discussed this with your own Insurance Company then it should be clear that <u>you were not at fault</u> or <u>not the main cause</u> of the accident.

Where it is <u>clear that you are not at fault</u>, then for accidents involving chain reactions and serious injuries, it will do <u>no harm</u> for you to agree to give a written statement.

This is information that you want the At-Fault Driver's Insurance Company to know.

<u>Insurance Settlement Secret # 39</u>

In practice, experienced Property and Injury Adjusters will only press you for a written statement where there are genuine doubts about liability and who caused the accident. This occurs where the claimant is fraudulently trying to make a claim.

No Collision Coverage
with your Own Insurance Company?

If you have no Collision coverage with your own Insurance Company then at this point you can request that the At-Fault Insurance Company pay for your vehicle damages.

They will open a property damage claim and arrange for your vehicle to have an **Appraisal** for damages.

At this point the At Fault Insurance Company Property Adjuster will ask you if you were injured. If you were injured tell them *"Yes"*.

If you are in doubt say *"Yes"*. This is because the At-Fault Insurance Adjuster will usually be calling you very soon, within hours or a few days after the accident.

Some types of injuries, especially soft tissue whiplash type injuries take a few days to show up. See section on **Soft Tissue Injuries** for more information.

Once you indicate to the at-fault driver's Insurance Company Property Damage Adjuster that you are injured, he or she will notify a separate **Bodily Injury Examiner/ Adjuster** in their company to be in touch with you.

How to Handle Yourself
When the Injury Examiner Calls

When the At Fault Insurance Company Injury Examiner calls, get his or her **name**, **address**, and **contact information**, including **telephone number**, **fax** and **e-mail**. Also write down the **Claim number** or **File number**.

This information will be very important for you to move your claim forward.

Insurance Settlement Tip # 11

Use as needed the Contact sheets at the end of this book to keep a record of your contacts with the At Fault Insurance Company Injury Examiner.

Remember when the other driver's Insurance Company Injury Examiner calls he or she will want to confirm that you are injured and wish to make an injury claim against them.

Typically you can expect to be asked a lot of questions about your injury. They will be trying to nail down if you <u>went to the Emergency</u>, or have an <u>appointment with your family doctor</u>.

If you followed through with the advice for step one, then you are ahead of the game. You can confirm that you are injured and that you went to the hospital and have an appointment with your doctor.

If you haven't gone to the hospital or doctor, the Injury Examiner may say nothing but later down the road questions will be raised why you delayed getting medical attention.

Insurance Settlement Secret # 40

It would be wise not to volunteer too much information here. Simply give general answers such as area of your injury (e.g. neck or back).

Advise the Injury Adjuster that it is **too early** to know the degree of you injuries and you will update him or her after you have fully recovered. This is perfectly reasonable given the nature of many injuries including *"soft tissue"* injuries.

The Injury Adjuster will send out to you forms to fill out. These usually include a **Bodily Injury Questionnaire** and **Medical and Employer Authorizations**. See samples at end of this book.

The Bodily Injury Questionnaire will ask you questions about your injury, your doctor's name, and whether you have pre-existing injuries or conditions and if you have lost work due to the injury. Your **Liability Claim** for injury is now <u>open</u>.

By this stage the At -Fault drivers' Insurance Company has acknowledged that you were in an accident involving their insured driver, that <u>their driver was likely 100% at fault</u> for the accident and that you are <u>injured</u>.

By sending out to you the Injury Questionnaire and Medical Authorization forms the At Fault driver's Insurance Company Injury Examiner is seeking to establish that your Injury was ***"as a result of the accident"***.

When you receive the Bodily Injury Questionnaire you should fill this out and return by mail along with a letter confirming the facts of the motor vehicle accident, that you are injured and that you are making an injury claim against the at fault driver's Insurance Company.

Insurance Settlement Tip # 12

See sample Confirmation letter for opening your

Liability claim in the *Insurance Settlement Secrets* Claims forms kit at the end.

This letter is just to establish in writing what you have already discussed on the phone. By sending the letter you are protecting yourself by giving them official <u>notice</u> of your injury claim.

This is exactly what a lawyer would do. It means that the At-Fault Insurance Company cannot later deny that they knew of your injury.

Medical and Employer Authorizations

If you sign and return the Medical Authorization and Employer authorization it means the at-fault Insurance Company Injury Examiner can write to your doctor for a medical report to get information on your injuries.

Insurance Settlement Secret # 41

Some auto accident injury claimants are absolutely against signing any medical or employer authorizations. Authorizations are simply gates through which information can flow. Whoever controls the authorizations controls the flow of information.

If you handle your own injury claim against the at-fault driver's insurance company then you control the flow of information. If you obtain representation then that person will control the flow of information.

Ultimately, if your injury was caused or aggravated by the auto accident you will want that information to reach the at-fault driver's Insurance Company sooner rather than later, so that your injury claim moves forward.

The **advantage** for you of **signing a Medical Authorization** for the Insurance Company is that if you need a medical report or documents as evidence of your injury and treatment to prove your case, the Insurance Company will obtain and <u>**pay**</u> for these for you.

The **disadvantage** is that the Insurance Injury Examiner may see a report showing other medical conditions unrelated to the motor vehicle accident.

If you wish to delay sending the Medical Authorizations and reserve the right to obtain and pay for medical reports yourself, you can do so. There will be more on this topic later.

The key point is that your Injury Claim is in play and you have sent a confirming letter with the filled out Injury Questionnaire. This gives the Insurance Company something to work with, and at the same time shows you mean business.

"Reservation of Right" Letter

Sometimes Insurance Companies send out a "Reservation of Rights" letter along with the Injury Questionnaire and Authorization forms. Do not be intimidated by this.

It just means the Insurance Company is protecting their rights and not accepting any liability until they have completed their investigation.

"Injury is not covered by their Insurance Policy"

In the **rare** case where the At-Fault Insurance Company Adjuster may not dispute that its Insured driver caused the Accident, but claims the accident is not covered by their Insurance Policy, there is a solution.

Insurance Settlement Secret # 42

Ask the At-Fault Insurance Company Examiner for the name of his/her **supervisor** or **manager**. There is always a manager or supervisor.

Write a letter to the Manager at the At-Fault Insurance Company stating you are giving them notice that you have been injured in an accident which was caused by their Insured driver and DEMAND a copy of their Insurance Policy showing that Liability is not covered.

Insurance Settlement Tip # 13

Use the same letter for confirming that you are opening a liability claim and **add the request for their Policy wording denying coverage**. For your protection it would be wise to send this letter by registered mail.

All States that require Automobile Insurance require at a minimum, Liability coverage. That is the whole point of Automobile Insurance, to protect innocent drivers.

Insurance Settlement Tip # 14

Look at your own Insurance Policy section on Liability. That will give you a good idea of the coverage the At-Fault driver has under his Policy. (See Automobile Insurance Policy section for more.)

Keep a copy of the letter for your records. It is very unlikely that the Insurance Company will maintain their denial of liability, since they have no right to do this where the facts show their driver was at fault.

If in the very unlikely scenario the Insurance Company maintains their denial despite the facts, you will learn ways to deal with this later in the book.

The key now for you is proceed to getting yourself recovered from your injury.

Stage ②

Medical Treatment and Rehabilitation

Congratulations on making it through the first stage. There was a lot of information to cover in stage one because that is where most of the crucial steps must be taken. Stage two is much easier.

The Rehabilitation stage or Medical Treatment stage is where your number one priority is <u>You</u> and getting yourself back to health and full recovery, just as you were before the accident happened.

Insurance Settlement Secret # 43

The first few weeks following the accident are <u>crucial</u> for documentation of an injury claim.

You must make the visits to the <u>Emergency</u> and to your <u>Doctor</u> as soon after the Motor Vehicle Accident as possible because reports of these visits can be ordered and will be <u>evidence</u> of an injury, whatever degree, and this translates into thousands of dollars for your settlement.

If you wait a month or two after the accident before seeking medical attention, then it will be much harder to show that your injury is related to the accident.

It is not impossible, but it makes it much harder to prove.

Remember, the purpose of this book is to help you make your injury claim **"bullet proof"** so that you get maximum dollars in your pocket for your insurance settlement.

Medical Treatment

The Emergency treating doctor will at the very least advise you to follow up with your own doctor. If the injury is significant, he/she may get you x-rayed immediately. If X-rays are done, then this is another report that can be ordered.

Also, after going to the Emergency and taking whatever treatment they recommend; muscle relaxers, pain killer, ice, heat, rest, etc., the Emergency doctor will advise you to follow-up with your family doctor.

(If you don't have one – request to get listed with a doctor).

Family Doctor

Your family doctor is on your side. He or she doesn't care about the Insurance Companies or litigation.

Your family doctor is there for you. This is your moment to communicate to the doctor any pain and suffering you are experiencing in the days and weeks and months following the accident, .

Insurance Settlement Secret # 44

The key here is to communicate. Why? Because your doctor will take notes (called **clinical notes**) and these can be requested by the insurance company as further proof of your injury.

Note: An observation--most women have no problem communicating but many men, especially young men, are very reluctant to talk about any physical pain, let alone go to a doctor.

Most young men could be black and blue with bruises and won't complain. That's okay on the football field or playing hockey, but if you don't talk to your doctor and spell out exactly the pain you have, then the doctor won't write it down. Then it won't be documented. Therefore, there will be no evidence of your injury.

If you tell your doctor *"I'm basically fine"*, he will write that down. How will that look on the report? That will look like you have recovered in a few days and it will cost you thousands of dollars in settlement. Being shy or macho here will cost you.

Insurance Settlement Secret # 45

If you are stuck for vocabulary, the keywords for soft tissue injuries are *"stiffness, sore neck, aching, neck hurts when turning, headaches, anxiety, can't sleep, etc."*

Note: Do not tell the doctor you have a *"soft tissue injury"*. That will sound like you are very claim conscious or have been coached by a lawyer and this may make him skeptical of you.
Just tell your doctor how you feel, where it hurts, etc. Let him examine you and make the diagnosis.

Insurance Settlement Secret # 46

Also communicate life disruptions such as that you can't do normal activities or you cannot socialize with friends etc.

You are 100% entitled to communicate to your doctors any aches and pains you have. It is your subjective opinion. Don't be shy. Spell it out to your doctor.

It is better to err on the side of more than less because it will give your doctor something to work with when he examines you.

The doctor will examine you and note his or her objective observations. The doctor will then write in the diagnosis: possible diagnosis are *"muscle spasms"*, *"strain"*, *"sprain"*, *"whiplash"*, *"whiplash grade I, II or III"*. He may indicate where, *"neck, left, right"*, *"shoulders"*, *"mid"* and *"lower back"*, *"soft tissue"*, *"injury"*, *"STI"*.

The Doctor will write in a prognosis, and may or may not give a time line. Doctors are cautious.

Insurance Settlement Secret # 47

Doctors must document and note all the details of your visit and they almost never state there is nothing wrong. They almost <u>always</u> state there is <u>something wrong,</u> otherwise why would you visit?

Note: If they are not sure they may state: *"Pending" or "under observation" or "prognosis guarded."*

Review: Why am I telling you all this medical information? Because you are pursuing an injury claim and it <u>must</u> be supported by medical documentation.

Remember the insurance injury examiner who ultimately will issue the check for your claim settlement will 99% of the time never meet with you in person. Therefore all he/she has to go on is medical reports and what you tell him or her.

Insurance Settlement Secret # 48

Keep your own medical treatment log and also document your subjective complaints. Once you have fully recovered and are back to normal activities it is very **easy to forget all the pain** and discomfort you have been through weeks or months ago.

If you keep a log of your *"pain and suffering"* and treatments then you will have lots of material for documenting your claim.

This material you can include in your <u>demand letter</u> when you are making your final settlement demand. This can increase your settlement by thousands of dollars.

This is the same technique that top personal injury lawyers use. They question you for all the details of your injuries and life disruption as a result of the accident and include this in their demand letter.

You will learn more about this later in <u>Chapter 22. Negotiating Your Settlement.</u>

Paying For Medical Treatment

In order to follow through with medical treatments you must be able to pay for medical treatments and expenses while your Third Party Liability Injury claim is pending against the At-Fault driver's Insurance Company.

Who will pay for your treatments and expenses depends on what type of insurance coverage is available to you.

Private Health Insurance

If you have Private Health Insurance on your own or through your Employer then they will pay for the treatments, usually up to a percentage such as 80%.

Either you pay the difference or you can go to your own Insurer for the difference. If the difference is still not paid then you can add this amount to your injury claim against the At-Fault driver's Insurance Company.

Medical Payments:

This is coverage under you own insurance to cover medical bills and expenses up to a certain dollar limit. This coverage also applies regardless of fault.

Medical payments coverage includes:

Family members of your household who were with you in your vehicle or another vehicle. It also covers anyone who was in your vehicle with your consent as a passenger or driver.

Not usually covered are motorcycles and vehicles owned by you but not listed on your insurance policy.

Also not covered are vehicles used in business, if not a passenger vehicle, as are accidents and injuries occurring while in the course of employment. The latter falls under Worker's Compensation rules.

You should refer to your Insurance Policy under the Medical Payments section, to see exactly what is and what is not covered.

Some Insurance Policies may require that you **repay** your Insurance Company for medical payments if you receive a settlement from the At-Fault driver's Insurance.

Insurance Settlement Secret # 49

Where your Insurance Policy requires that the Medical Payments you receive be reimbursed if you receive a Liability Injury settlement, you may be better off using your general Health Insurance or other coverage instead.

Personal Injury Protection (PIP or "No Fault")

In states with No-Fault Insurance laws, this type of coverage will pay for your medical expenses no matter who is at fault for the accident.

Therefore if you were injured in an accident caused by another person you would claim your medical expenses from your own Insurance Company.

Where more than one person is responsible for the Accident

Where more than one person is responsible for the accident and your injuries, you may have access to more than one insurance policy to cover your damages.

Chain reactions and multiple vehicle accidents are where this situation normally arises.

In this case, if one of the insurance policies has insufficient coverage for all your damages, then this policy will provide *"Primary"* coverage and the other at-fault driver's insurance policy will cover the shortfall under *"Secondary"* coverage.

Insurance Settlement Secret # 50

You don't have to worry about who is primary or secondary. All you have to do is give both at-fault insurance companies notice of your claim against them and these insurance companies will sort out between themselves who is primary and secondary and let you know.

Passengers

What if you are not the driver of the vehicle involved in the accident, but rather you were a passenger?

If you were injured and you were a passenger then you can open two Third Party Liability claims. You can open a claim against the Insurance coverage of the driver of the vehicle in which you were a passenger, and also open claims against the driver/owner of any other vehicles involved in the accident.

Note: You cannot collect the full amount from both insurance policies.

However, if one driver's insurance coverage is insufficient, you can make up the shortfall from the other policy coverage.

Insurance Settlement Secret # 51

If you are an injured passenger you will also need immediate coverage for your medical bills and expenses. Passengers should file a claim for Medical Payments coverage with their own Automobile Insurance coverage. Again, Medical Payments coverage is not based on fault.

Your Liability claim(s) for pain and suffering should still proceed against the driver of the vehicle or the at-fault driver of the other vehicle, or both.

Insurance Settlement Secret # 52

Where your Liability claims are against more than one at-fault driver, you can collect the whole amount of your damages from any one of them, but not more than the full value of the claim.

Last Resorts for Paying Cost of Treatment

If you have no Private Disability Insurance, and you have no Medical Payments coverage through your own automobile Insurance Policy, there are two other options:

1. Pay up front for emergency visits, doctor visits, medications and course of treatments but keep all the receipts.

2. If you have absolutely no Health Insurance Coverage and cannot afford to pay up front for these medical bills, remember there is a solution.

Ask the At-Fault Insurance Company to Pay

Contact the Insurance Injury Examiner of the at-fault driver's Insurance Company, against whom you have opened a Liability Injury Claim.

Refer to your contact sheet. You will have the name and contact information of the person because immediately after the accident they, or their independent insurance adjuster, will have contacted you for statement and to see if injured, etc.
If you cannot afford to pay for medical visits and treatment, tell the Insurance Examiner and ask him or her if they will be willing to pay for your course of medical treatment.

Insurance Settlement Secret # 53

Many at-fault Insurance Companies will agree to pay up to a certain amount for treatments if you confirm in writing that you have no other coverage and they have already established that their driver was at-fault.

Why? Because, the at-fault Insurance Company knows that their insured driver caused your injury and it is in their interests that you get better and return to normal as soon as possible otherwise they know this could prolong your injury or loss and make it worse and then they may have to pay a larger settlement.

The legal term for this is **mitigation.** If you have tried all you could to reduce your loss then it cannot be held against you that you could not afford to get more treatments.

Also, if you are hurt you need to get some treatment so as not to end up with a permanent chronic injury.

Doctor's Referrals

The At-Fault Insurance Company Injury Examiner will usually ask for a copy of the referral note from your family doctor referring you for physiotherapy, chiropractic treatment, medications, etc.

You can fax a copy of the doctor's referral note to the Insurance Company Injury Examiner. You can then go to a physiotherapy clinic and advise the clinic to contact the at-fault insurance company examiner to confirm they will pay for a course of treatments.

The Physiotherapy Clinic will then contact the Insurance company who will request a progress report before authorizing more payments.

The At-fault driver's Insurance Company is doing exactly what your Private Health Insurance or your own Insurance Company would do under Medical Payments or PIP coverage.

Insurance Settlement Secret # 54

It is possible that the Injury Examiner may try and offer a quick settlement and get you to sign a release. Do **not** do this. It is too

93

early.

<u>Advise</u> the examiner that you need to do the treatments first and follow-up with your doctor before making any settlement.

If the examiner refuses to cover treatments, you can advise him or her that if treatments will not be covered, then you have no choice but to go to a lawyer. Give the name of the lawyer.

(See section on <u>Last Resort: Hire a Personal Injury Lawyer</u>).

If you are uncomfortable, on the next page there is a sample letter you can fax to the examiner to cover medical expenses and treatments.

There is also another sample letter for requesting treatments at the end of the book.

Note: Send this only after confirming you have no Private or Employer coverage and that you have no coverage for Medical Payments through your own auto insurance.

Remember, you should only approach the At-Fault Insurance Company to cover treatments if you absolutely have no other medical benefits.

Most Automobile Insurance Policies include some form of Medical Payments coverage for payment of your medical bills as a result of a motor vehicle accident, regardless of who was at fault.

SAMPLE LETTER REQUESTING PAYMENT FOR MEDICAL EXPENSES

Your Name
Your Address

Your Telephone #
Other contact Information

Date

Bodily Injury Examiner
At -fault Driver's Insurance Company
Address

Dear Injury Examiner:

Re: Your Insured Driver: (At-Fault Driver's name)
Your file #:

I was injured in a motor vehicle accident on _____ date, which was caused by your insured driver.

I have been referred for treatments by my doctor (referral note copy attached). I have no private health insurance and no benefits through my employer and no coverage through my own automobile insurance company.

Please confirm that your company will pay for medical treatments as soon as possible. Please also be advised that if you do not assist in treatment coverage you will leave me no choice but to have a lawyer contact you.

I look forward to hearing from you.

Sincerely,

x Your Name

This letter sample is only as a last resort when you have exhausted all other avenues for paying for treatment.

The bottom line, it is important for you to follow-up on treatments to get back to health, at least as you were before the accident.

If you do not follow-up with your treatments, it could prolong recovery and also make it harder to show you were really injured.

Note: If you are injured, it is **your responsibility** to take steps to get better and recover.

By sending a letter requesting payment for your medical treatments when you have exhausted all other avenues, it shows you are doing all you can and it puts the pressure on the at-fault driver's Insurance Company to help you.

If they don't help you with your treatment costs, then if you later get a lawyer they could have a much larger settlement exposure.

No-Fault States

Almost half the states in the United States have some form of No-Fault Insurance. This will be referred to in your Insurance Policy as **Personal Injury Protection (PIP).**

The purpose of no-fault coverage is to avoid liability claims for smaller accidents. In exchange, the injured person's own insurance company will pay for the medical bills and lost income as a result of the accident.

No-fault does typically still not apply to vehicle damages, which are handled separately either by your own insurance company if you have collision, or by the at -fault driver's insurance company if you do not.

The problem with No-Fault coverage is that while it pays promptly for medical bills and lost income without any arguments about liability, it provides no compensation for *"pain and suffering"*.

Also in states with no-fault the PIP benefits vary. Sometimes PIP benefits fail to reimburse fully the injured person for medical costs and income loss.

You need to check your individual Automobile Insurance Policy to see the exact amount of PIP benefits you carry. They usually have a set dollar limit and/or a set time limit from the date of the accident to collect coverage.

As you can see the Insurance Industry has clearly benefited from No-Fault systems because they reduce their costs for liability disputes and at the same time reduce their pay outs.

However, even with the No-Fault states all is not lost for pursuing the At-Fault driver's Insurance Company for pain and suffering.

Insurance Settlement Secret # 55

Since PIP benefits do not cover everything, you can still file a Liability claim against the at-fault driver, even in no-fault states.

Your Liability claim would be for any medical costs and income loss above what your received from PIP benefits as well as general damages for pain and suffering and other special damages. This operates in the same way as Liability claims in states that do not have "no-fault" laws.

Each no-fault state has different specific requirements for pursuing a liability claim against the at-fault driver on top of your PIP coverage with your insurer.

Add on States

Some no-fault states have no restrictions on your right to file a liability claim for damages in excess of your PIP coverage.

Monetary Threshold States

Once you have reached the medical expense threshold under the PIP coverage, then you are free to pursue the at-fault driver's Insurance company with a liability claim.

Insurance Settlement Secret # 56

Medical expenses threshold can be reached quite quickly with the rising costs of medical care and services.

The general rule is that all necessary medical expenses as a result of the accident are included to meet the threshold, but you need to check your policy wording to see exactly what is included.

Many no-fault states have quite low limits for pay out even under PIP, so the threshold should not be hard to meet.

States or Provinces with a very generous No-fault system, such as Ontario, Canada make it more difficult to reach the threshold, but not impossible.

Serious Injury Threshold States

Some No-Fault states only allow an injured person to pursue a liability claim for pain and suffering if the insured person suffered a *"serious" injury* ".

Each No-fault state with a *"serious injury"* threshold will have different definitions of serious injury.

Example of these *"serious"* injury definitions include:

"Permanent disability", "permanent impairment", "significant permanent use of an important part or bodily function", "Substantial scarring or disfigurement", "permanent injury", "permanent loss of a body function", "Serious impairment of an important bodily function", "60 days disability", "some disability or full disability over 180 days", "significant limitation of body function or system", "substantially full disability for 90 days".

As you can see the definitions of *"serious"* injury vary widely.

Insurance Settlement Secret # 57

It is well known in the Insurance Industry and the legal community that these definitions of *"serious"* injury are so vague as to be almost meaningless.

A capable personal injury lawyer would be able to get around these vague definitions in court and show that you meet the threshold.

The Insurance Companies know this and therefore will **take very seriously your liability claim**, even in no-fault states and even if you don't have a lawyer yet.

Insurance Settlement Secret # 58

Do not be intimidated by these thresholds even if you are diagnosed with soft tissue injuries.

In no-fault states with a *"serious"* injury threshold it is not difficult to get your doctor to write a report giving you a 1-3% permanent impairment to push you into the threshold.

Soft tissue injuries are known to last for years and can be very debilitating.

Finally, some no-fault states have a combination of both a *"monetary"* and *"serious injury"* thresholds before allowing liability claims.

If you live in no-fault state or your accident occurred in a no-fault state you will need check your policy for exactly what the PIP coverage is and what are the thresholds for making a liability claim.

Where The Motor Vehicle Accident Happened in a No-Fault State

Where the Motor Vehicle Accident happened in another state the general rule is that the law of the state where the accident happened applies.

However, this does **not affect your Insurance Coverage**.

Therefore, if you had an accident in a state with No-Fault Insurance but you live in a state without no-fault laws, then you can pursue your injury claim for full compensation just as in your own state.

This is because the at fault driver's Insurance Company must honor all valid claims against their Insured driver.

Since you don't have the benefit of no fault coverage in your state you need to receive full compensation for your injury as a result of the accident.

Insurance Settlement Secret # 59

Laws governing insurance frequently change. It is important that you have current information for your state or province.

Your own Insurance Policy will have all the information your need including definitions but you can also obtain current information at your State Department of Insurance web site.

Insurance Settlement Tip # 15

The National Association of Insurance Commissioners (NAIC) web site lists links to all the State Department of Insurance web sites.

See http://www.naic.org

"Soft Tissue" Injuries

The most common types of injuries as a result of car accidents besides cuts, bruises and fractures are actually *"soft tissue"* injuries.

"Soft Tissue" injuries are injuries to the muscle fibers and tissue as opposed to bone fractures. The usual location for these injuries is the neck area (cervical spine), shoulders, upper back and lower back (lumbar spine) areas.

The problem with *"Soft Tissue"* injuries is that they are not outwardly visible injuries, unlike cuts, bruises and fractures. For this reason many people, including traditionally the Insurance Industry, have assumed that *"Soft Tissue"* injuries are less serious than visible injuries such as fractures.

The courts have taken a different view. Modern medicine has shown that *"soft tissue"* injuries are very real injuries and can be much more serious than even fractures, which usually heal within weeks.

"Soft tissue" injuries often take much longer to heal and can become chronic and even permanent.

Faced with the reality of courts now recognizing "Soft tissue" injuries, the Insurance Industry has had to move away from the traditional view and treat *"Soft Tissue"* injuries as more serious injuries.

What is a "Whiplash" injury?

Much medical literature has been written about *"Soft Tissue"* injuries especially Soft Tissue injuries to the neck area. These are commonly known as ***"Whiplash"*** type injuries.

They involve a sprain or strain type injury to the muscles along the upper back and neck. A normal x-ray of the neck shows a certain curvature of the cervical spine.

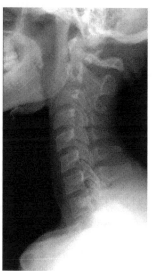

A whiplash injury typically involves tension in the muscles and soft tissues of the neck and cervical spine. This can result in an abnormal curvature of the spine forward or a straightening of the spine at the neck. This is known as *"loss of the normal lordotic curve"*.

The most recent trend in medicine and the Insurance Industry is to classify *"Soft Tissue injuries"*: Mild, Moderate or Severe. *

(See *Quebec Task Force on Whiplash Associated Disorders)

Statistics show that these are very common types of injuries that are seen arising out of motor vehicle accidents.

Modern technology has resulted in automobiles that have become able to absorb shock .

Vehicles with plastic bumpers and softer metal that have been in a collision may appear to have no damage or very minor damage.

However, crash studies have shown that the actually impact on the human body in the seated position can be very traumatic, even at low speeds.

Accident Reconstruction studies have shown that the human body is first pulled back when a vehicle is hit from behind then the head and neck are thrust forward and back again creating tremendous strain on the cervical and lumbar spine.

The effects of the impact may be immediate or may take days to appear.

The results of such an injury can result in stiffness, strain or sprained neck. This can be very painful and debilitating.

There is loss of mobility, pain and often headaches at the base of the skull. The medical term is *"occipital pain"*.

You may have difficulty sleeping. The prolonged nature of this type of injury can very detrimental to your well being and you may become very stressed and even depressed.

Even with aggressive treatment such *"Soft Tissue"* injuries usually take a minimum of months to heal and often last several years.

Another problem with these *"Soft tissue"* injuries is that they can easily be re-aggravated in the workplace or at home.

Many people who work at desk jobs in front of a computer can experience re-aggravation of these injuries. This can be very frustrating, debilitating and very discouraging.

If your job involves heavy lifting such as for physical labor jobs, nursing and personal care workers, then soft tissue injuries can easily be re-aggravated and require more treatments.

All this pain and suffering and yet outwardly such injuries are not visible.

Compare a fracture injury such as a broken leg or arm with very visible cuts and bruises and a cast. Such injuries while serious, usually heal in a few weeks and the injured person is soon up and running and back to normal with no long term consequences.

How will you know how serious your injury is?

Only you and your treating doctors will know and they will only know after examining you and monitoring your treatment over a period of time.

Many injuries can develop into serious injuries even though at first they appear minor. This is especially true for soft tissue injuries that may not become a problem until several days or weeks after the accident.

Treatments

Traditional treatments for "Soft Tissue" injuries have been rest, heat, and ice, medications such as anti-inflammatories, muscle relaxants, pain killers, as well as courses of treatments at physiotherapy clinics, and/or by more modern trend, chiropractic treatments, massage treatments and gym and home exercise programs.

Your doctor will also refer you for some of these treatments: rest, ice, heat at a minimum as well as muscle relaxants and pain killers.

Your doctor may request x-rays, suggest some time off work, and refer you for physiotherapy or massage.

Another option for treatment is to go to a chiropractor. Chiropractors are medically trained and offer treatments for soft tissue neck and back injuries that have helped a lot of people.

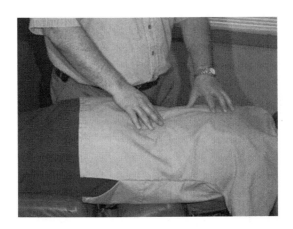

Note: Some medical doctors see chiropractors as competition and may not recommend them.

A chiropractor's report may not have as much weight before the bodily injury insurance examiner's eyes, because the examiner will look to the diagnosis of the family doctor.

Also, chiropractors, like physiotherapy clinics and massage therapists have an economic interest in keeping you going for treatments.

Therefore, Insurance Injury Claims Examiners are more skeptical of chiropractors' and physiotherapists' diagnosis.

However, despite this chiropractors can produce detailed reports of treatments and injuries which can be used as more evidence should you ever go to court. The insurance companies know this.

Insurance Settlement Secret # 60

It is better to have a referral from your Family Doctor before beginning a course of treatment whether for physiotherapy, Chiropractor or massage.

This is because the Injury Examiner will review your medical documentation to see if you really were referred for treatment by your doctor.

If you decided to do physiotherapy, massage treatment or attend a chiropractor on your own without consulting a doctor and without a referral, it weakens your claim that your injury was a result of the motor vehicle accident.

Remember, you want to make your injury claim **"bullet proof"**, so that it cannot be attacked in court by defense lawyers for the Insurance Company.

The at-fault driver's Insurance Company will not wish to argue with a referral for treatment by a doctor.

Review – You went to the Emergency, then you followed up with your family doctor, you started physiotherapy, or chiropractic treatment or massage, and have been taking medications.
All this is evidence of injury and that you are taking steps to get better.

How Long Will It Take To Recover and Start Settlement Negotiations?

Normally with *"whiplash type"* injuries they take from a few months to a few years to resolve. It depends on the degree of *"whiplash injury"*.

Each individual and injury are different. Most car accident injuries are strains and sprains to neck, shoulders and back. The only person who can monitor the pain is you. It is your responsibility to get treatment to get well.

There are around 3 million injuries as a result of automobile accidents every year according to the United States Department of Transportation statistics.

This means there are a lot of injury claims being handled by Insurance Companies and lawyers.

Although for you the injured person, the injury claims process is a very personal and traumatic experience, for the Insurance Company Injury Examiner and the lawyers it is simply a job.

Insurance Company Injury Examiners and the lawyers look at your injury from a cold financial perspective.

Part of their cold analysis is to create cutoff periods.

Insurance Settlement Secret # 61

The following are usual cutoff periods often referred to by the Insurance Industry and the courts.

"Nuisance" Claims

Little or no treatment and fully recovered within a **few weeks**.

Minor Claims

Six months is the approximate cutoff period for minor claims in the eyes of the Insurance Companies and to some degree, the courts.

If you have fully recovered and all treatments have ended within six months of the accident, then this would generally be described as a minor injury claim.

If you are fully recovered to how you were pre-accident proceed to Stage Three and the Negotiation Process.

Small Claims

The third cut off period for injury settlements is whether your injury has resolved and you have fully recovered within approximately **1 year** of the accident.

A small injury of whiplash type or soft tissue should have mainly resolved by 1 year or so.

Please note what the Insurance Industry describes as *"Small"* Claims does not mean small dollar amounts.

(See the sections on How to Calculate the Value of Your Injury Claim and Negotiating Your Settlement.)

Monitoring and Protecting you Legal rights

As you are approaching the 1 year mark following the accident you will need to monitor your legal options.

See the next section on State Statutes of Limitation.

More Serious Injury Claims

1 Year – 18 months Post Motor Vehicle Accident

If you are still undergoing treatment beyond 1 year from the accident or you are still off work, then your injury is more severe than the average soft tissue injury and you should receive a higher settlement.

Insurance Settlement's Secret # 62

Since whiplash and soft tissue injuries can last and flare up again for several years and can also be re-aggravated by work, it is imperative you don't settle and sign the final release too early.

If you do, then this lets the Insurance Company off the hook and you cannot recover any more from them.

Consult with your doctor. Ultimately you and only you will know when you have fully recovered to your pre-accident form.

Insurance Settlement's Secret # 63

If you are still undergoing treatments after 18 months post accident, this suggests a serious injury and your injury claim may require the services of a lawyer to help you negotiate large dollar amounts.

Large Loss Injuries

Any type of head injury should be thoroughly looked into by your doctor for neurological damage.

Serious head injuries can have long term consequences and for proper compensation you may need the services of an experienced personal injury lawyer.

See the section Last Resort: Hire a Personal Injury Lawyer.

Statutes of Limitations

A Statute of Limitations is simply a set time limit to file a legal action.

Any lawsuit arising from an accident or injury must be filed within a certain time limit or the injured person's legal claim will be barred and his or her right to sue will be lost forever.

Every State has enacted its own Statutes of Limitations, requiring any personal injury suit be filed in court within a set time after the incident or injury.

The Statute of Limitations in each State ranges from one year to six years. The average is 2 years.

At the end of this section is a list of the Statute of Limitations Periods for each State.

Insurance Settlement Secret # 64

State Legislation changes frequently and this can include Statute of Limitation periods. If in doubt, check your own State's Department of Insurance.

Or;

Call the Claims Department of your own Insurance Company and ask them what the Statute of Limitation period is for bringing an action for injury. Your own Insurance Company will tell you.

The Statute of Limitations period for bringing an action is important and you should be aware of the time limit in your state.

However, if you follow through with the 3 Steps to settling your injury claim, your claim will most likely be settled long before the Limitation period expires in your state.

If you are approaching the expiration, and for some reason the At-Fault Driver's Insurance company refuses to settle with you, then you should consider hiring a personal injury lawyer who can arrange for your claim to be filed with the court.

Insurance Settlement Secret # 65

To file an action with the court to meet the Statute of Limitations period, simply contact a personal injury lawyer. (See Section <u>Last Resort: Hire</u> <u>a Personal Injury Lawyer</u>) A personal injury lawyer can file an action with the court within 24 hours.

The purpose of Statute of Limitations is to protect the at fault drivers and their Insurance Companies from being *"prejudiced"* by any delay.

An example of such prejudice would be where the Insurance Company was unable to investigate the scene of the accident or important evidence was destroyed.

It is up to the Insurance Companies to prove any prejudice caused by delay.

Insurance Settlement Secret # 66

In practice, it is difficult for Insurance Companies to prove they have been prejudiced by delay.

Also, since the Insurance Company was notified by its own Insured driver of the accident and you have opened a claim with them and have <u>sent letters</u> to them and vice versa, the Insurance Company cannot claim two years down the road that they didn't know about your claim.

Most Automobile Injury Claims <u>Can be Settled</u> Before the Limitation Period Expires.

The majority of automobile injuries are soft tissue injuries and of those most have resolved within a year or 18 months. Most Statute of Limitation periods give you 2 years or more to bring an action in court.

Remember: If you follow through with the 3 Steps to settling your Injury claim it will be <u>unlikely</u> to get to this stage when the facts show the other driver was at-fault and you have been in settlement negotiations with the at-fault driver's Insurance Company.

However, in a few states the Stature of Limitation period is shorter and you will need to be aware of this to protect your rights should your injury prolong or the negotiation process break down.

Motor Vehicle Accidents in Another State

As you have learned, if the Motor Vehicle Accident happened in another state the general rule is that the law of the state where the accident happened applies.

This means that you should be aware of the Statue of Limitation period in the **state where the accident happened**.

Below is a list of State Statute of Limitation Periods for bringing Personal Injury actions.

Alabama
2 years   (Ala. Code Sec. 6-2-38)

Alaska   (Alaska Stat. Sec. 9.10.070)
2 years

Arizona   (Ariz. Rev. Stat. Sec. 12-542)
2 years

Arkansas   (Ark. Stat. Sec. 16-56-104)
1 year

California   (Cal. Code of Civ. Proc. Sec. 335.1)
2 years

Colorado
3 years
(Colo. Rev. Stat. Sec. 13-80-101(n))

Connecticut
3 years
(Conn. Gen. State. Sec. 52-577)

Delaware
2 years
(Del. Code Ann. Title 10, Sec. 8119)

District of
Columbia
1 years
(D.C. Code Ann. Sec. 12-301(4))

Florida
4 years
(Fla. Stat. Ann. Sec. 95.11)

Georgia
2 years
(Ga. Code Ann. Sec. 9-3-33)

Hawaii
2 years
(Haw. Rev. Stat. Sec. 657.7)

Idaho
2 years
(Idaho Code Sec. 5-219)

Illinois
2 years
(Ill. Ann. State. Ch. 5, Sec. 13-202)

Indiana
2 years
(Ind. Code Ann. Sec. 34-11-2-4)

Iowa
2 years
(Iowa Code Ann. Sec. 614.1)

Kansas
1 year
(Kan. Stat. Ann. Sec. 60-514(b))

Kentucky
1 year
(Ky. Rev. Stat. Sec. 413.140)

Louisiana   (La. Civ. Code Ann. Art. 3492)
1 year

Maine   (Maine Rev. Stat. Ann. Art. 14, Sec. 753)
2 years

Maryland   (Md. Cts. & Jud. Proc., Sec. 5-105)
1 year

Massachusetts   (Mass. Gen. Laws, Art. 260, Sec. 2A, 4)
3 years

Michigan   (Mich. Comp Laws Sec. 600.5805(2))
2 years

Minnesota   (Minn. Stat. Ann. Sec. 541.05, 541.07)
2 years

Mississippi   (Miss. Code Ann. Sec. 15-1-35)
1 year

Missouri   (Missouri Ann. Stat. Title 35, Sec. 516.140)
2 years

Montana   (Mont. Code Ann. Sec. 27-2-204)
3 years

Nebraska   (Neb. Rev. Stat. Sec. 25-208)
1 year

Nevada   (Nev. Rev. Stat. Sec 11.190)
2 years

New Hampshire   (N.H. Rev. State. Sec. 508.4)
3 years

New Jersey   (N.J. Stat. Ann. Sec. 2A:14-2)
2 years

New Mexico
3 years

(N.M. Stat. Ann. Sec. 37-1-8)

New York
3 years

(N.Y. Civ. Prac. R. Sec. 214)

North Carolina
3 years

(N.C. Gen. Stat. Sec. 1-52)

North Dakota
2 years

(N.D. Cent. Code Sec. 28-01-18)

Ohio
2 years

(Ohio Rev. Code Sec. 2305.10)

Oklahoma
1 year

(Okla. Stat. Ann. Title 12, Sec. 95(4)

Oregon
2 years

(Ore. Rev. Stat. Sec. 12.110)

Pennsylvania
2 years

(42 Pa. Con. Stat. Sec. 5524)

Rhode Island
3 years

(R.I. Gen. Laws Sec. 9-1-14)

South Carolina
2 years

(S.C. Code Ann. Sec. 15-3-550)

South Dakota
2 years

(S.D. Comp. Laws Ann. Sec. 15-2-15(1))

Tennessee
1 year

(Tenn. Code Ann. Sec. 28-3-104)

Texas
2 years

(Tex. Civ. Prac. & Rem. Code Sec. 16.003)

| Utah
1 year | (Utah Code Ann. Sec. 78-12-29(4) |
| West Virginia
2 years | |

Utah
1 year   (Utah Code Ann. Sec. 78-12-29(4)

Vermont
3 years   (Vt. Stat. Ann. Title 12, Sec. 512)

Virginia
2 years   (Va. Code Sec. 8.01-243)

Washington
2 years   (Wa. Rev. Code Ann. Sec. 4.16.100(1)

West Virginia
2 years   (W. Va. Code Sec. 55-2-12)

Wisconsin
2 years   (Wis. Stat. Ann. Sec. 893.57)

Wyoming
1 year   (Wy. Stat. Ann. Sec. 1-3-105(a)(v), (B)

Note:

This information is a guide only. State Legislation changes frequently. Check your own State's Department of Insurance for current Limitation Periods.

Stage 3

Evidence to Support Your Injury Claim

Congratulations on making it through stage 2. If you have followed through with the logical steps of Stage 1 and 2 of opening your different claims and doing medical treatment, you are in a very strong position to proceed through stage 3 and successfully negotiate your injury claim settlement.

You Must Be Fully Recovered from your Injury

Note: You must be certain that you have <u>fully recovered</u> to the same condition you were in before the accident happened before starting the Negotiation stage.

The test is whether you are still undergoing active treatment. If you are, you must complete all treatment related to the accident before proceeding.

Stage 3: Collecting Evidence to Support Your Injury Claim

As stated previously, the only information the Injury Claims Examiner has to determine the value of your claim is through the <u>documentation</u> that you provide or make available.

Medical Evidence

By going to the Emergency, your Doctor and following a course at the treating clinic, there will be a <u>documentary trail</u> to support that your were injured as a result of the accident.

For *"Nuisance Value"* injury claims, where you had only a very slight injury and did no treatment you may feel you don't need to bother with getting a medical report.

It is true that the Injury Examiner will likely take your word that you have been to the Emergency. In fact, the Injury Claims Examiner may not even request a copy of the report.

However, you should be aware that even one medical report from the Hospital Emergency can bump up the value of your settlement by another thousand or two dollars.

Insurance Settlement Secret # 67

Once the injury examiner has at least one report on file showing you suffered some type of injury after the accident, the examiner's authority on how much your potential settlement could be is immediately increased by thousands of dollars.

Even if the Emergency Record simply states that you had a very mild injury and to go home and take Tylenol, the Injury Examiner will take this seriously because this is still evidence to support your injury in court.

Therefore, it is in your financial interest to make sure the Injury Claims Examiner has the documentation to support you injury.

You may be asking if you have to pay for this medical report.

This is a legitimate question and you have three options.

1. You can order an Emergency Report from the Hospital and pay for this yourself and add this amount to your injury claim demand.

2. You can ask the Injury Claims Examiner if the Insurance Company will pay for medical reports. Then order an Emergency Report from the Hospital and send the report with the invoice to the Insurance Company.

The advantage to options 1 and 2 is that you can see and can make copies of reports you obtain before you send them to the Injury Claims Examiner. This gives you more control.

3. You can allow the Injury Claims Examiner to write directly to the Hospital or your doctor for reports if you have signed the Medical Authorization Form that was sent to you just after you opened your Injury Claim.

The disadvantage of this approach is that you will likely never see the Emergency or Medical report and you will also have to confirm that the Injury Examiner has ordered and received the documents.

Insurance Settlement Tip # 16

Injury Claims Examiners handle many claims at a time so you should call and leave messages asking the Examiner to confirm he or she has received the report.

Remember to be polite and quote your file or claim number.

Some argue you should never sign the Medical Authorization Form because the reports may reveal information you do not wish revealed.

In my opinion, this is only relevant if you have something to hide. You should not worry about this if you are completely honest when making your claim.

If you have a prior history of injuries from motor vehicle accidents or a degenerative medical condition, this will be revealed. Injury Claims Examiners have a sharp eye for details like this.

However, even where you have a medical history of previous motor vehicle accidents and or injuries, it still cannot take away the fact that you were injured or suffered an aggravation of a prior injury as a result of the motor vehicle accident.

Insurance Settlement Secret # 68

Injury Claims Examiners are not really interested in seeing your past Medical History before the accident. They are really just looking for documentation that supports your injury and record of treatment as a result of the motor vehicle accident.

It is only where there are inconsistencies, such as the medical reports you or your representative provide do not give full details or adequately explain the degree of your injury, that the Injury Claims Examiner must request and examine lots of Medical reports and Doctor's Clinical notes to review and separate fact from fiction.

By signing a Medical Authorization, you enable the Injury Claims Examiner to obtain the medical documentation for you, to **support your claim**.

It is to your benefit that the Injury Claims Examiner believes you. The only way he or she will believe you is if they can see the "documents".

Another reason you don't have to worry about what is in an Emergency Report or a Medical Report from your doctor is that you were there at the time. You know exactly what you said and what the doctor advised you.

Also, you will have taken notes and documented these visits in your Medical Treatment Logs provided at the end of this book!

Insurance Settlement Secret # 69

The Hospital Emergency Record may cost from $50-$100.

A Medical Report from your doctor can range from $50 to around several hundred dollars depending on the doctor and the degree of detail.

What is the Injury Examiner looking for in the Medical Reports?

The Injury Examiner is looking to confirm 2 things.

1. That you really did suffer an injury as a result of the motor vehicle accident.

2. How serious is your injury and whether you were referred for treatment or were put off work.

Emergency Record

Emergency Record reports like other Automobile Accident reports are Medical forms containing specific sections.

These Medical Report Forms will contain basics like your name, date of birth, the date and time of the medical visit, and importantly will refer to the motor vehicle accident.

In the comments section there is space where the Emergency Doctor will make notes:

1. The SUBJECTIVE COMPLAINTS section is where YOU describe how you are feeling and where it hurts and you have pain. Here the doctor will write down exactly what you tell him or her.

It is very important to tell him that you were in an accident and to describe any stiffness or pain you subjectively feel.

2. The doctor will examine you and then write down his OBJECTIVE OBSERVATIONS.

3. In the next section there is a box labeled: DIAGNOSIS. This is where the Emergency doctor uses professional judgment and describes your injury in medical terms:

E.g. *"Fractured femur"*, *"Mild Muscle Spasm"*, *""Soft Tissue Injury to neck"*, *"Cervical strain"* *"Lumbar sprain"* *"Whiplash"* etc.

The DIAGNOSIS box is the most important information on the Emergency report for You. I will go into more detail later.

4. The RECOMMENDED TREATMENTS section is where the doctor makes a referral for medications, or to see family doctor, or if more serious, for x-rays.

5. The last box is usually called PROGNOSIS. This is where the Doctor gives an estimate of how long your injury should last.

This is the least important section on the Emergency record because this the first time you have seen a doctor for the injury and he or she can only be vague. This is only an impression and the prognosis can change by the time of your next visit or treatment.

As you can see there is a lot of detail even in a simple Emergency Record.

Insurance Settlement Secret # 70

The Injury Examiner is really interested only in the DIAGNOSIS, RECOMMENDED TREATMENT AND PROGNOSIS.

He or she simply needs to confirm the facts of your injury and will likely only glance at the report, make a note and put it in the file.

The Injury Examiner will only scrutinize closely your Emergency Record if there is something that doesn't make sense, such as you are having excessive treatments not associated with that type of injury.

Also if you stated to the Doctor that you still managed to play a round of golf after the accident, this may show up in the comments section and is relevant to the seriousness of your injury.

Medical Reports from Your Doctor

Medical reports from your doctor are more in the form of a narrative letter which documents your subjective complaints, objective findings on examination, diagnosis, referrals for treatment and prognosis.

If you have a history of visits and treatments, then a detailed medical report from your doctor would describe the sequence of your visits and your progress since the accident.

Insurance Settlement Secret # 71

A very good source of documents to support your injury claim is your Private Health Insurance, if you went through them or through your own Insurance Company under Medical Payments Coverage.

Your Insurance Company or your Private health Provider can only release records of what Medical Treatment coverage your received, if you authorize this.

You can authorize release of records by sending a separate letter to the Injury Claims Examiner or to your Insurance Company agreeing to release of the records.

The advantage for you is all the records will relate only to treatments you have received in relation to the motor vehicle accident. Also you won't have to pay for these records.

Another option is for you to keep receipts from the clinics and medications paid and photocopy them and submit this with your demand letter.

Documenting Loss of Income

If you were put off work by your doctor for any time as a result of the motor vehicle accident injury, you can claim income loss as part of your injury claim.

The Injury Examiner will need to see some documentation from your doctor confirming this and for how long.

Also you will have to provide a letter from your Employer stating the dates of work and how much wages or salary you lost.

If you wish the Injury Examiner to write for this you will have to sign an Employer Release of information Authorization.

Self Employed

It is more problematic to show loss of income for self employed people. In this case if you can send reasonable documentation of income earned for months prior to the accident this should suffice.

Remember honesty is the best policy for all claim demands.
The key point is that it is in your interests to accurately document your losses as this makes it much easier for the Injury Claims Examiner to agree to your settlement demand.

All the Injury Examiner is looking for is documentation to support the figures your are asking for.

Inside the Insurance Company

I am now going to take you inside the Insurance Company against whom you have a liability claim. This is real inside information.

I have worked for years doing just injury claims. Every year I settled hundreds of claims for all types of injuries arising out of automobile accidents.

I have also decided and have published many legal decisions for Workers Compensation injury cases.

Why is this important to you?

Because having real information about how the at-fault driver's Insurance Company you are dealing with handles the injury claim process, is worth thousands of dollars to you.

The At-Fault Driver's Insurance Company

Like most people you probably imagine the Insurance Company which is likely a billion dollar company to be an intimidating faceless monolith out to deny your claim at any cost.

The reality is that for most Insurance Companies this could not be further from the truth.

Insurance Settlement Secret # 72

The modern trend, where liability is clear, is to make every effort to accommodate and settle your (the injured party) claim quickly and not waste large amounts of money on investigation and surveillance, etc.

There are a few large older Insurance Companies that are slow to change and are clinging to old approaches of spending thousands of dollars (more than the claim is worth) trying to deny at all costs. But these few companies are losing money big time as well as market share.

Also, I will show you exactly how to handle the few companies out there who use the old approach.

Insurance Settlement Secret # 73

The modern trend for insurance companies is to operate by Telephone Call-Centers either on a regional or national basis. I am sure you are familiar already with the names of some of these companies.

Modern insurance companies, in order to be more efficient, try to have specialists take care of each type of claim.

Therefore, a Property (Vehicle) Damages Adjuster will have called you and taken care of the damages to your vehicle (if not done by your own insurance company because you did not have collision coverage), and someone else, an Injury Claims Examiner will call you and talk with you about your injury claim.

Insurance Settlement Secret # 74

The person you are dealing with for your injury claim is working at a desk or cubicle with a phone headset on.

The Injury Claims Examiner

This Injury Claim Examiner sits in front of a computer all day and has piles of files on or near his or her desk.

At the same time he or she is handling your claim, he or she is handling hundreds of other claims for injured parties.

Every day they get large bundles of mail with medical reports and letters from lawyers with demand letters and threats of lawsuits.

The Injury Examiner usually has a lot of experience and is skilled at analyzing and making decisions on injury claims. The Injury Examiner will probably be responsible for millions of dollars.

However, despite the difficulty and responsibility, these Injury Claims Examiners are overworked and do not receive a high salary.

Insurance Settlement Secret # 75

Across the insurance industry there is a very high burn out rate for Injury Claims Examiners (known in the industry as Bodily Injury (BI) analysts). The more efficient a person becomes, the more and more claim files they are given.

When the experienced skilled Injury Examiner finally quits (eventually most do) after 2-5 years because of physical health deterioration or mental exhaustion, the Insurance Company hires someone else.

This is standard across the Insurance Industry.

As a result, for injury claims arising from automobile accidents, Insurance Companies never seem to have enough people to handle all injury claims. They always are playing catch up, rather than investing in hiring more people.

One of the problems is the job requires a lot of insurance, medical, legal and analytical experience as well as an ability for technical know-how.

As a result of this, insurance companies are often **desperate to close** claims and cut down the number of files open. Some insurance companies may offer bonuses to these Injury Examiners just to close files.

Why is this important to you?

The fact that you now know that the Injury Examiner at the other end of the telephone is <u>very anxious </u>to settle, puts <u>You</u> in the <u>advantage</u> and gives you *leverage*.

<u>Insurance Settlement Secret # 76</u>

As a general rule, insurance adjusters are very happy, if not downright **desperate to close files** and the only way they can do so is to reach settlement.

Their managers often judge the injury adjuster's performance on the number of files they close.

<u>Insurance Settlement Secret # 77</u>

The **longer you wait to settle** your injury claim, **the more pressure is on the Injury Examiner to close the claim** and the file, which means the Injury adjuster becomes more and more <u>desperate to settle</u> the claim.

So you are thinking, okay, that's fine, I have to deal with one person, the injury adjuster, and I have to be patient, but how does the system work?

You need some more details. How do you get your check? Will there be enough money? How will you know what to ask for?

Insurers Insider Secret # 78

The Injury Examiner will set aside sufficient funds for your settlement as soon as you open a claim.

That's right, as soon as you confirm to the injury adjuster that you are injured, the Insurance Injury Examiner with the at-fault driver's Insurance Company sets aside thousands of dollars to pay for your claim.

The law requires Insurance Companies have sufficient funds set aside to pay claims. This figure to be set aside is decided by actuaries higher up in the Insurance Company.

The money the Injury Claims Examiner sets aside has a technical term. It is known in the Insurance industry as a <u>RESERVE.</u>

You don't need to remember this word. All you need to know is that when you are seeking settlement, you are not just asking for money from their big bank account.

Instead, by setting up a reserve amount, the Insurance Company Injury Examiner already knows and has a general range of how much your settlement could be worth.

The key is that your settlement claim <u>money is already</u> <u>set aside</u> to pay you the moment you open your claim.

As more information comes in from you on the degree of injury that amount is adjusted upwards.

For example, if your doctor recommends several months of

physiotherapy treatment, the Injury Claims Examiner knows your injury will last at least several months and will set aside money accordingly.

Insurance Settlement Secret # 79

There is another trend in the Insurance Industry. In order to cut down even more on the cost of handling claims, Insurance Companies are setting up Offshore offices to handle claims.

Even though the Insurance Company may have an <u>Independent Adjuster</u> meet with you locally and do an on-site investigation, there is a good possibility that the person really handling your claim is actually not in your State or even in the United States.

The Injury Examiner may be actually calling you from Bangalore, India and speaking in a trained American accent.

This is just to give you some perspective on how the Insurance Companies view liability claims.

To the Insurance Companies, you are just a number and your claim is just a cool business calculation.

Insurance Settlement Secret # 80

Once liability has clearly been established, the At-Fault Driver's Insurance Company simply <u>processes</u> your claim as if on a factory assembly line.

For most auto accident injury claims the process is <u>not rocket science</u>.

You fill in the blanks with documentation of your losses, the Injury Analyst adds it all up, an offer is made and you and the Insurance Company reach settlement.

The only thing that people outside the industry don't have is exactly what elements can be added to increase the value of your settlement.

The Insurance Companies rely on your not knowing in order to keep your settlement figure down and they keep the profits.

It is to the advantage of the Insurance Companies to give the impression that it is a complex and intimidating process.

See the sections on <u>How Much the Insurance Company is Willing to Pay</u> and <u>How to Calculate the Value of Your Injury Claim</u> for more details.

Insurance Settlement Secret # 81

Finally, there is one bit of information that will be very useful to you and give you real leverage when it comes to negotiating your injury settlement.

The *"Achilles Heel"* of the Insurance Companies

Insurance Companies collect billions of dollars every year in premiums which are paid in advance. Losses do not occur at once and are spread out over the policy year.

This means that the Insurance Companies have large pools of capital available to <u>invest</u>. Insurers invest heavily in Federal and State government bonds and also in the stock market.

Government regulations specify the types of investments permitted to Insurance Companies but there is still considerable flexibility.

How does this affect you and your injury claim?

As long as your injury claim is open the Insurance Company must have tens of thousands of dollars, or hundreds of thousands for large claims, set aside in RESERVES.

While this money is tied up in reserves it cannot be used in investments. It must be liquid and available to pay your claim.

If you multiply your claim by the thousands of injury claims one single Insurance Company handles each year, as well as the fact that many injury claims remain unresolved for years, this amounts to hundreds of millions of dollars.

This is money that the Insurance Company cannot invest and use to earn more income.

This means that for every injury claim open, not only does the cost of the paying your injury claim keep rising, but the Insurance Company is also losing profit income for not investing the money tied up in Reserves.

This is the Achilles Heel of Insurance Companies. Their prime reason for existence is to make a profit.

Therefore, if you hold firm to your claim demand and are patient, the Injury Examiner will think nothing of bumping up their offer by 5 or 10 thousand dollars in order to close the claim.

The Insurance Company decision is not just based on the value of your injury claim but on a cold calculated business decision of how much money they are losing while your claim is open.

Knowing the *"Achilles Heel"* of the Insurance Company will put you in a powerful negotiating position when finalizing your settlement.

Review Points:

1. You are dealing with an Injury Examiner who is just one overworked underpaid human being who has full responsibility and authority to settle your claim and issue you a check.

3. Your Injury Claim is processed just like in an assembly line.

3. Have patience. The longer you wait to settle, the higher the dollar value of your settlement.

How The Negotiation Process Works

One of the most common questions I received from claimants in my years handling injury claims was *"What is the status of my claim?"*

This is a legitimate question. However....

Insurance Settlement Secret # 82

When you ask about the status of your claim it indicates to the Injury Examiner two things:

1. You don't know much about how the claims process works.
2. You are ready to settle your claim.

It is nothing personal against you the claimant but the Injury Examiner wants to get the file closed as soon as possible.

When you ask about the status of your claim, the Injury Examiner will gently suggest that you must be feeling better and basically recovered. After all, if you were still undergoing serious treatments you would not be calling about the status of your claim.

You likely are feeling better and want to get things settled and that is why you have called but you have now shown your hand. Your call about the status shows you are ready to settle.

The Injury Examiner will ask you if you are interested in bringing your claim to a conclusion and settlement and may ask how much you are looking for. The Injury Examiner will likely advise you they will review the medical documentation on file and call you back. The negotiating process has begun.

This is great if you truly are ready to settle. However, typically claimants ask about the status of their claim too soon after the accident, when they are even still doing treatment.

Also, the Injury Examiner is now leading you through the negotiations and not the other way around.

The purpose of this section of the book is to guide you through the settlement process so that you really look like you **know what you are doing** and the Insurance Company will take you much more seriously.

Also, I will show you how to take the lead in the negotiation process.

The combined effect will result in much higher settlement amounts for your injury claim. The difference will be in the thousands of dollars.

How Much is Your Claim Worth?

When you are injured in an automobile accident caused by someone else, the general rule is that the at-fault person is liable for all the "reasonably foreseeable" consequences that flow from the accident.

This includes: Medical expenses, loss of income, pain and suffering etc.

There may also be consequences such as loss of social or educational opportunity, loss of consortium with family, emotional stress and future costs.

There may have been costs for housekeeping while you were recovering. Also, depending on the degree of injury, there may be future costs for care and housekeeping.

If you have some permanent injury and you are disabled from work, the loss of income calculation can be substantial.

As you can see, there are lots of items to add up.

Insurance Settlement Secret # 83

Simply by showing the Injury Examiner that <u>you know exactly how much the claim is worth</u> will put you in a very strong bargaining position.

Insurance Settlement Secret # 84

The Injury Examiner will have no problem agreeing to your settlement demand if you can <u>substantiate</u> your claim with reasonable evidence.

All the Injury Examiner wants to do is close your file as soon as possible and get it off his desk. All he or she needs is the documentation to substantiate the numbers, then there will be no problem issuing a check.

The Injury Examiner needs the proof so that when he or she is audited by their superiors they can justify the settlement money is well spent.

The problem is most injured claimants have no idea how to calculate the value of their claim.

How the Negotiation Process Usually Works in the Real World

You, the injured claimant, don't know how to calculate the value of your claim, so you present a number to the Insurance Company but have very little to back it up. The number may be too high or it may be too low.

Either way it shows the Injury Examiner you don't know what's going on.

The Insurance Injury Examiner seeks a detailed breakdown to substantiate your demand and you, as the claimant, don't know exactly how to do this. You become frustrated and either accept a much lower amount or you hire a personal injury lawyer.

Once the claimant hires a personal injury lawyer, the whole claims process is **put on hold** for a year to several years.

Eventually, a year or two later, your lawyer sends in a **demand letter** to the Insurance Company. Typically the demand letter is for a very high dollar amount and an immediate response is requested.

The overworked and underpaid Injury Examiner reviews the file and requests the documentation to back up the demand.

In my experience, the personal injury lawyer almost always **holds back some information**, such as statements for determining liability, medical documentation and proof of income loss, hoping that the Insurance Company Injury Examiner will not notice and also to use the missing information as a bargaining chip.

If the Injury Examiner is experienced and diligent he or she will persist in getting documentation from your lawyer before agreeing to any demand.

Once the Injury Examiner receives the information, he or she will send a **counter offer**.

In most cases, from my years of experience dealing with auto accident injury claims, eventually the evidence does **not** support the higher dollar amount they are seeking.
Examples of evidence not supporting the facts of the claim:

1. Demand letters claiming thousands of dollars in past and future income loss, when the evidence shows the claimant didn't miss a day from work and their doctor said they were able to work.

2. Demand letters claiming very large amounts when the evidence eventually shows the claimant wasn't even injured and had no treatment as a result of the accident.

3. Even a demand letter claiming that a client's loss of her leg was due to the accident. Eventually the evidence showed the leg was lost years before the accident due to other causes.

All the while legal costs and fees are rising for all the hours spent sending letters for medical reports and making calls etc.

From my experience, many personal injury lawyers, as part of their negotiation tactics on behalf of their client and knowing that the Injury Examiner is swamped with claims and demands, will leave multiple telephone messages and send faxes, often with threatening language.

Experienced Injury Examiners are not swayed by this but at the same time they are human beings and this puts them under a lot of stress. Especially, when they received dozens of threatening letters and messages each day.

As part of the negotiation process it is standard to threaten the insurance company with court action unless the Insurance Company agrees to a set dollar figure. The more aggressive the lawyer, the higher the dollar amount.

At this point the Insurance Injury Examiner has to make a decision.

Either accept the higher dollar amount demanded on behalf of the injured claimant and close the claim, or send the file to the Insurance Company Defense Counsel.

Insurance Settlement Secret # 85

This decision is a **cold business decision** and not based on the actual merits of the claim. The Insurance Injury Examiner knows that Defense costs will be thousands of dollars extra even if it never goes to trial.

Therefore, the Injury Examiner makes a cold calculation whether it would be cheaper just to agree to the claimant's demand, or if in the long run it would be cheaper to send it to Defense counsel, even with the extra legal costs.

The end result is that, behind the scenes of your Injury Claim, the

Insurance Company is <u>paying thousands of dollars extra</u> in legal costs, and you may know nothing about this.

Why is this important to you?

This is many thousands of dollars that the Insurance Company is <u>willing to spend</u> to close the claim and yet only a <u>fraction</u> is going to you the injured person.

Example:

Let's say you had a mild injury with some income loss and you feel your claim is worth $10,000. You don't know how to calculate this figure so the Insurance Company offers you $5000.

You threaten to go to a lawyer so the Insurance Injury Examiner offers you $7500.

Either you accept this because you know that even if you get $10,000 the lawyer will take around $2500 in fees, or you decide to hire a lawyer anyway.

You decide to hire a lawyer who tells you not to worry and that you will get your $10,000.

If it is getting close to the Statute of Limitation expiration date in your State the lawyer will file papers with the court to protect your rights.

Your lawyer writes to your doctor for a medical report and sends a demand letter (often months or years later) to the Insurance Company Injury Examiner handling your claim.

The demand letter is seeking a higher number such as $50,000 or more in damages for your claim.

The Injury Examiner makes a counter offer, based on the limited evidence he or she has on file so far, say $12,500 to settle your claim.

The lawyer wants more than this because after deducting legal fees you will get less than $10,000.

Your lawyer rejects the counter offer and forces the Insurance Company to hire Defense counsel.

Insurance Settlement Tip # 17

The legal process is that your lawyer files a <u>Summons and Complaint</u> with the court and <u>serves</u> papers on the <u>at-fault driver</u>. This obligates the Insurance Company to hire their own lawyer to defend against the legal action on behalf of their insured at-fault driver.

The Insurance Company lawyer begins the defense process by filing with the court.

Lawyers are busy with hundreds if not several thousand files, and your claim gets **put on hold again** for several months.

Your lawyer will be asked by the Insurance Company Lawyer to produce more evidence.

You may be called for a *"Deposition"* and questioned by the Insurance Company lawyer. It is learned at the Deposition and with the medical evidence that you were not seriously injured.

In the end, you were right about the value of your claim. It was really worth around $10,000.

Insurance Settlement Secret # 86

You, the injured person, know better than anyone else your claim details and exactly how serious your injury is.

The Insurance Company, using its lawyer, finally agrees to settle for $15,000 to make your lawyer happy so he gets his fees and costs.

You get your $10,000. Your lawyer gets $5000 in fees and costs. The Insurance Company lawyer also gets $5000-$10,000 in fees.

This is on top of the several thousand in expenses the Insurance Company paid to investigate the claim and order medical reports.

What's wrong with this picture?

You were the person injured but out of almost $30,000 that the Insurance Company actually paid to close the claim, you only received $10,000.

This example is typical of what happens in Insurance Industry. Insurance Companies often pay out large amounts of money before a claim is settled and yet only a fraction of that goes to the injured person.

Read on and I will show how you can potentially receive a settlement of $20,000-$25,000 in a claim like this instead of just $10,000. This way You, the Injured person will be happy and even the Insurance Company will be happy because it will have saved time and money.

Insurance Settlement Secret # 87

In the majority of auto accident injury cases there is no need for any lawyers to be involved at all in the process.

Why? Two reasons:

1. Once liability and causation are clearly established, the at-fault driver's Insurance Company will never go to trial because they know they will lose.

As you saw in the section on Liability, most vehicle accidents fit into standard accident scenarios and liability is not difficult to establish.

Also, the issue of whether an injury was caused by the accident can be established in most cases very easily with medical documentation.

2. If the <u>only issue is amount of damages</u> there are much better options than going to trial. Trials are very expensive and time consuming.

<u>Mediation</u> and <u>Arbitration</u> are popular ways to resolve differences and reach settlements.

But even Mediation and Arbitration cost thousands of dollars to set up in addition to the legal fees for both sides. The Insurance Companies have no choice but to pay these costs just because lawyers are involved.

Insurance Settlement Secret # 88

All this huge extra cost is because of two things:

1. You, the injured person, don't know how much the Insurance Companies are **really prepared to pay** for your injury claim.

2. You don't know how to **calculate the value of your injury claim**.

Read on to learn very valuable **Insurance Settlement Secrets.**

How Much the Insurance Company is Willing to Pay

Across the Insurance Industry there are variations in calculating the value of Bodily Injury claims. There is no magic formula.

However, trained Bodily Injury Examiners use standard techniques to narrow down the process to as much of a science as possible.

I am now going to reveal inside information that is known by very few people outside the Insurance Industry and legal world.

Insurance Settlement Secret # 89

In the Insurance Industry Bodily Injury Examiners use special worksheets generally called **Bodily Injury Reserve Worksheets**.

There are variations across the Insurance industry and each Bodily Injury Claims department may draw up their own unique format.

However, whatever the format, Bodily Injury Reserve Worksheets contain certain key elements.

These fall under the two main headings of GENERAL DAMAGES and SPECIAL DAMAGES.

General Damages refer to *"Pain and suffering"*.

Special Damages refer to specific medical expenses, income loss and other quantifiable expenses.

Below are Damage headings commonly used by Bodily Injury Examiners to determine the value of your injury claim.

Most of these headings you will be able to include in your demand letter. (More on how to write your Demand letter later.)

Hospital and Medical expenses:

This includes things like still <u>unpaid</u> Ambulance Bills and other hospital expenses.

Loss of Income:

If you are off work due to being injured in a motor vehicle accident then you can claim against the At-Fault Driver's Insurance Company.

All you have to do is be able substantiate the loss. You can do this by having your Employer send a letter stating the time you were off and how much wage loss you missed.

If you received wage loss benefits from a Private Health Insurance Plan or through your own Insurance, then all you can claim is any shortfall difference.

In some states you can only claim Net lost income instead of Gross. However, it certainly won't harm you to claim gross lost income in your demand anyway.

Medical Payments Received:

As stated earlier in the Medical Payments and Treatment section, you may be required to <u>repay</u> your Insurer or Private Insurance Coverage for any Medical Payments benefits you received. If you are required to pay this then <u>include</u> this figure in your demand letter.
Remember, if you are required to pay this amount back then it is really <u>separate from your own injury claim</u> and should be <u>in addition</u> to your general damages claim for pain and suffering.

Insurance Settlement Tip # 18

Another option for you is to request in your demand letter that the At-Fault driver's Insurance Company issue a separate check directly payable to your Insurance Company that is seeking reimbursement.

144

(See <u>How to Calculate the Value of Your Injury Claim</u>)

GENERAL DAMAGES

The general damages heading is the heart of your claim. Technically general damages refer to your *"pain and suffering"* only.

This is what confuses a lot of people. How can you put a dollar amount on *"pain and suffering"*?

<u>Insurance Settlement Secret # 90</u>

The answer is you cannot really put a price on pain and suffering. The best that professional Insurance people and lawyers can do is make a calculated guess.

That calculated guess varies from state to state and company to company, and is influenced by several factors including the degree of your injury, recent case law, the size of your community etc.

There are different formulas to make the calculation, but even the formulas allow a lot of room to negotiate.

However, I will show you how this calculation is made in the Insurance Industry so that you are on the same page as they are and they will see that you know what your are doing.

The 1.5 - 5 x Damages Formula

One formula followed by many Insurance Injury Examiners is to **multiply** the amount of special damages, i.e. the amount of **Medical Payments you received or paid for, by 1.5 - 5**.

Therefore, with **"nuisance" value** claims you may use **1.5 - 2.5**. For **minor injuries** multiply by **3 - 4.5** and for more **serious injuries** multiply **5** times the Medical Payments paid.

This formula is never revealed by the Insurance Injury Examiner. As you can see there will be quite a range of difference between

145

one and a half and five times the special damages.

Obviously the more serious the injury the higher the number of multiplication that you would use.

Insurance settlement secret # 91

Another more simple formula that I have <u>successfully</u> used for many years is based on my experience on the values of injury claims.

"Rule of Thumb" Formula

A *"rule of thumb"* is to multiply the <u>number of months</u> of treatment <u>until</u> <u>full recovery</u> following the accident by $1000.

> Example: If your injury lasted 6 months you could claim $6000 in general damages. If your injury lasted one year to 18 months your general damages would range from $12,000 to $18,000.

Remember, your injury lasted **as long as you continued to have pain and suffering** and were still receiving any form of medical treatment.

As you saw in the section on <u>Soft Tissue Injuries</u>, some Insurance Injury Claims Examiners regard *"soft tissue injuries"* as less serious than fracture type injuries. This is not the case.

The modern trend is to treat soft tissue injuries as serious, if not more serious, due to the fact that they can take much longer to heal and can be easily aggravated in the workplace or at home. They can also be very painful, debilitating and can become chronic.

Permanent Injuries

Where there is a diagnosis of a permanent injury or an indication in the medical report that you will have recurring or degenerative future problems this will indicate a much more serious claim.

Special Note for Head Injuries.

Injuries involving recurring headaches and dizziness or involving concussion and periods of unconsciousness could indicate much more serious injuries including neurological damage and it is especially important to communicate these complaints to your doctor.

It is impossible to know immediately after the accident, sometimes until weeks or months later, the degree of injury you have suffered.

If the diagnosis is serious you will have to consult a personal injury lawyer as this could involve long term consequences for you and you will need assistance in negotiating settlement.

(See section: Last Resort: Hire A Personal Injury Lawyer)

Housekeeping

It is possible that you will have had some expenses for housekeeping during your period of disability. This is a common heading under special damages.

Emotional Distress

Other than physical pain and suffering, you may be entitled to other types of loss for trouble sleeping, eating, upset stomach, side effects to medication etc.

Injuries as a result of motor vehicle accidents can cause stress, embarrassment, depression and strains on family relationships, such as inability to look after children, and other problems.

Life Disruption

Another consideration in your claim can be for loss of opportunity, including social and family functions and educational opportunities.

e.g. If you are unable to attend a family wedding because of your injury from the motor vehicle accident then this *"loss"* should be stated in you demand letter.

Future Care

The cost of Future Care cost is often presented in the demand letter of personal injury lawyers. The Insurance Company will consider a figure under this heading if there is some indication in the medical evidence that the claimant may need some additional care.

Even where there is no indication of this in the evidence, a small figure of $1500 may be considered.

This heading is almost always included in the demand letter of personal injury lawyers simply to give some room for negotiation.

Future Lost Income

Where an injured claimant has suffered a degree of impairment from their injury which forces them to find alternative work or that completely prevents them from working, a figure for Future Lost Income can be included.

This can amount to substantial sums. Often the claim for Future Lost Income as a result of a permanent injury can be higher than the claim for general damages.

Where substantial sums are involved for Future Lost Income it is usually to your advantage to have a personal injury lawyer represent you in the negotiations.

Legal Costs

Statutory fees, hourly fees, filing fees, additional expenses and costs of the personal injury lawyer will be factored in by the Injury Claims Examiner if your are represented.

Insurance Settlement Secret # 92

A figure for potential legal costs will be factored in <u>even if you don't have a lawyer</u>, as there is always the possibility that you may do so. This is important for you to know when you present your settlement demand letter.

(Independent) Adjuster Fees

This is where the Insurance Company hires an Independent Adjuster on the location to do certain tasks such as obtain statements, photographs, talk to witnesses etc.

Private Investigation Fees

Where fraud is suspected a private Investigator may be hired to do video surveillance. A few days of surveillance can quickly add up to several thousand dollars in fees.

Medical Reports

A figure is included to cover the costs of obtaining medical reports, either directly to the doctor or hospital or to reimburse the claimant or their personal injury lawyer.

Pre-judgment Interest Specials

Since your claim could takes months or years from the date of the motor vehicle accident before settlement is reached, most jurisdictions award the settlement amount for specials plus interest multiplied by the number of months to settle.

Each jurisdiction may have different formulas. A typical example is 2.5% interest on the total of the special damages.

This is divided by 12 (months of the year) . Then this figure is multiplied by the exact number of months since the date of the accident or loss.

Pre-judgment Interest Generals

A figure for prejudgement interest is also calculated for the general damages award.

Defense Costs

If a claimant hires a personal injury lawyer and a legal action is filed and served on the at fault driver, his or her Insurance Company will have to hire Defense Counsel.

Defense work for Insurance Company claims is very lucrative and the Insurance Companies pay large amounts in defense costs.

This figure is even higher than the (plaintiff counsel) personal injury lawyer costs. Again this figure is factored in for calculating the Reserve, even if the claimant is not yet represented.

The total of these figures is added up to give the Injury Examiner an estimate to set the Reserve to cover the costs of the claim.

Insurance Settlement Secret # 93

The Bodily Injury Reserve Worksheet will be attached to the file and the Injury Claims Examiner will revisit these figures several times throughout the life of the claim.

When the file comes up for review and new information is received the Examiner will adjust upwards the potential exposure and increase the Reserves.

On the next page is a Sample Bodily Injury Reserve Worksheet.

The figures are for illustration purposes only.

You can see different columns showing the amounts adjusted upwards after the Injury Examiner reviews your claim file and the resulting increased total RESERVE amounts.

BODILY INJURY ADJUSTER RESERVE WORKSHEET

CLAIMS #_____ Insured _____

CLAIMANT (YOU) _____ Age___ Marital Status__

Occupation _____ Employer _____

Nature of Injuries:_____

_____

Date of Loss: _____ Attorney: _____ Seat Belt: Yes ( ) No ( )

Prognosis and Disability: _____Date: _____

DAMAGE HEADINGS	Date	Date	Date
Hospital			
Medical			
Loss of Income	$2500	$2500	$2500
Medical Payments	$1800	$1800	$2200
GENERAL DAMAGES	$7500	$12500	$17500
Housekeeping	$1500	$1500	$1500
Future Care	$1500	$1500	$2000
Future Lost Income	0		0
Legal Costs	$1750	$1850	$1950
Adjuster Fees	$2000	$2000	$2000
Private Investigation Fees	0	0	0
Medical Reports	$750	$1050	$1100
Pre judgment Interest Specials	$200	$250	$250
Pre judgment Interest Generals	$350	$375	$400
Defense Costs	$5000	$5000	$5000
Total	$24,850	$30,325	$36,400
RESERVES	$30,000	$50,000	$75,000

Insurance Settlement Secret # 94

Compare the figures for the GENERAL DAMAGES for *"pain and suffering"* with the total RESERVE amount at the bottom of the column.

Notice how the GENERAL DAMAGES amount is substantially less than **what the Insurance Company expects to actually pay** out for the claim.

This is real exclusive Insurance Settlement information.

How to Calculate the Value of Your Injury Claim

When you are injured in a motor vehicle accident which was CAUSED, (or mainly caused) by someone else, then the VALUE or WORTH of your injury claim is based on the <u>consequences</u> that result from the accident.

The CONSEQUENCES flowing from that accident include your <u>injury pain and suffering</u>, your <u>medical expenses</u>, <u>loss of income</u>, <u>loss of opportunity</u>, <u>household costs</u>, <u>future care costs</u>, <u>life disruption costs</u>, even <u>emotional costs</u>.

The Insurance Company for the at fault driver has a CONTRACT (Automobile Insurance Policy with Third Party Liability Coverage) to pay for all these consequences that flow from the at-fault driver's actions.

As you saw in the previous chapter on how the Insurance Company puts a value on the injury claim, the consequences can add up.

How much is <u>your</u> injury claim worth?

<u>Insurance Settlement Secret # 95</u>

Here is the key **<u>Insurance Settlement Secrets</u>^{TM} formula** for your injury claim:

> **Total of your SPECIAL DAMAGES + your GENERAL DAMAGES + the COST the Insurance Company is willing to pay to close your claim.**

As you learned earlier, the Insurance Companies stand to profit when they can get you to settle your injury claim for less than they are prepared to pay.

They get away with this because most people have no idea how much they are really prepared to pay.

As you learned in the previous section, you now know what the Insurance Companies are prepared to pay and actually do pay.

Insurance Settlement Secret # 96

If you can demonstrate in your demand letter that **you know** how much the Insurance Company believes your claim is worth and how much they are prepared to pay, they will fold and agree to your settlement.

Insurance Settlement Secret # 97

The easy way to demonstrate that you know the value of your claim is simply to include a breakdown with different damage headings in your demand letter just like the Bodily Injury Examiner does on the Bodily Injury Reserve Worksheet.

The key is that once THEY KNOW that YOU KNOW how the process works, their advantage is lost . They have no other option but to pay.

You have the advantage. You know their position. Let's proceed to put a value on your injury claim.

Step 1.   Add up all your SPECIAL DAMAGES.

This is the easiest step. All you have to do is collect the receipts you have for medical expenses, invoices from treating clinics and the Record of total Medical Payments received either through your Insurer or Private Health coverage, and records of Income Loss. Then add these all up.

Hospital and Medical expenses:

Receipts for Ambulance Bills and other medical expenses that you had to pay yourself. E.g. Medications that you had to pay for yourself.

Medical Payments:

Total amount of Medical Payments received either through your Insurer or Private Health coverage which you are obligated to repay.

(If you don't have to repay Medical Payments received then you have already received compensation for this and cannot claim this amount twice.)

Loss of Income:

Total loss of income or wages. Losing sick days or vacation days is considered the same as losing pay. If you received sick pay or took vacation days and actually did not lose income this is irrelevant.

You have lost that sick time or vacation time and are entitled to claim it.

If you lost overtime hours and can show that your were scheduled to work these hours then include this figure in loss of income.

Housekeeping

Total receipts of your expenses for housekeeping during your period of disability. E.g. Paying someone to come in and clean the house, mow the lawn, deliver groceries etc. Any expenses that you would not normally have to pay.

Loss of Opportunity Costs

If you were enrolled in a course that you had to stop because of your injury, include the cost of the course. You will need to back this up with a receipt or invoice of the amount you paid.

If you were unable to attend a wedding or graduation, include out of pocket expenses.

Future Care

The cost of Future Care where you doctor has <u>recommended</u> some additional care. E.g. gym membership or medication.

A small amount of $1000-$1500 can be included.

Future Lost Income

If you have suffered an injury with a degree of permanent impairment which forces you to find alternative work or that completely prevents you from working, a figure for Future lost income can be included.

This can amount to substantial sums. Often the claim for Future lost income as a result of a permanent injury can be higher than the claim for general damages.

Where <u>substantial sums</u> are involved for future lost income it is usually to your advantage to have a <u>personal injury lawyer</u> represent you in the negotiations.

Medical Reports

Include any amount you had to pay for the Hospital Emergency Record and medical reports.

Step 2.   Calculate your GENERAL DAMAGES

As you know general damages refer to your *"pain and suffering"* only.

As you learned in the previous section many Insurance Company Injury Examiners use the **1.5 - 5 x Medical Payments Damages Formula**.

As you can see there is a big difference between multiplying the amount of Medical Payments costs by 1.5 instead of by 5 times.

Insurance Settlement Secret # 98

An easy way to put a <u>value</u> on your injury claim is to look at 2 factors:

1. The Category of Injury Claim

Injury claims are classified in the Insurance Industry as **Nuisance, Minor, Small** and potential **Large Loss Claims.**

2. The Degree of Injury

Medical reports will often describe the degree of injury especially *"soft tissue"* and *"whiplash"* type injuries.

The degrees are: MILD , MODERATE and SEVERE. They may also include "GRADE I, II, or III".

The following is a <u>sample guide</u> to show you the different claims categories and what the value is in the minds of the Insurance Industry.

Case law is constantly changing. This information is not cast in stone and is just to give you signposts or markers when calculating your <u>general damages</u>.

Remember, <u>You,</u> more than anyone else will know exactly what type of injury you experienced.

"Nuisance" Value Claims

Any injury claim that settles for $5000-$6000 or less is considered a *"Nuisance Value"* claim across the Insurance Industry. In larger centers this figure could be higher.

The Injury Examiner will often immediately offer you an nominal amount of $500 -$1000.

Insurance Settlement Secret # 99

If you hold off on settlement for 3 months the value of your claim goes up. Just having your injury claim still open is costing the Insurance Companies money.

If you wait 3 months to settle your injury claim most Insurance Companies will not blink at paying you up to $2500 to settle and close your claim, even without any medical reports.

If you had little or no treatment and have fully recovered within a few weeks, but wait 3 months before settling and provide an Emergency report or report from your doctor confirming you suffered an injury as a result of the accident, the value of your claim goes up several thousand dollars.

If your injury claim is still open six months after the motor vehicle accident, and there is a medical report on file confirming an injury, most Insurance Companies will think nothing of settling this for up to $5000.

Remember this figure is only general damages. If you have receipts and records of Special damages then this figure can be added to the total.

Minor Claims

In the Insurance Industry any injury claim that settles for under $15,000 is considered a minor claim. In some larger centers this figure could be higher.

Six months is the approximate cutoff period for full recovery for minor injury claims in the eyes of Injury Claims Examiners, Personal Injury Lawyers and to some degree, the courts.

If you have finished all treatments within 3 months of the accident and are fully recovered by six months, then this would generally be described as a minor injury claim.

Example 1: A typical course of physiotherapy from a Doctor's referral for a soft tissue injury is 15 treatments. i.e. 2-3 times per week for 4-6 weeks.

A second course of physiotherapy treatments of 4-6 weeks will take you to approximately 3 months post accident.

Multiply the total Medical Payments cost by 3.5 to get your range.

Or you can use the **"Rule of Thumb"** to multiply the number of months until full recovery with no complaints following the accident by $1000. Choose whichever figure is higher.

Small Claims

An injury claim from an automobile accident that settles for $30,000 or less is almost always considered by Insurance Companies as a *"Small Claim".*

Again, this is just a guide. In larger centers this figure could be much higher.

You should be fully recovered and not have any more complaints or flare-ups by 1 year post accident.

Remember *"Soft tissue"* can take a long time to heal. Also there can be flare-ups months down the road and you can have a relapse and have to do more treatment.

Compare a fracture and broken limb injury where although you are laid up for a few weeks, you may be fully recovered and out playing sports again within a couple of months.

Multiply the total Medical Payments costs by 5 to get your range.

Or you can use the **"Rule of Thumb"** to multiply the number of months until full recovery with no complaints following the accident by $1000.

Choose whichever figure is higher.

Typically a doctor's diagnosis of *"Moderate"* injury *"Grade I or II"* will be indicated on a medical report.

Insurance Settlement Secret # 100

You should give yourself six months after you have completed an extended course of active treatments to be certain you don't have a flare-up later and that you are fully recovered.

Remember you need to make sure your are fully recovered before you attempt to settle. Once you reach settlement and sign the Final Release, that's it.

You have some discretion here. If you have documented in your Medical Treatment Logs lots of detail of pain and discomfort then you should include this in your Demand Letter and request the higher amount. (See next section.)

If you don't have much detail to put in your demand letter to bolster your injury claim then you may want to err on the lower end.

Remember we are only calculating your General Damages at this point.

Insurance Settlement Secret # 101

If your injury hasn't completely resolved within 1 year from the date of the accident and you are still undergoing active treatment then you may have a more severe injury and a large claim.

You should consult an personal injury lawyer. See section Last Resort: Hire a Personal Injury Lawyer.

Step 3: Add 30%-40% to your total for General Damages.

This is the amount you learned in the previous section that the at-fault driver's Insurance Company is really **willing to pay** to avoid Legal costs and their own Defense costs.

Include the 30-40% in your figure for General Damages but **do not** reveal that you added this in your breakdown. It will be understood by the Injury Examiner.

Sample Breakdown

Special Damages:

Hospital and Medical expenses..$

Medical Payments to repay..$

Loss of Income...$

Housekeeping...$

Loss of Opportunity Costs...$

Future Care..$

Future Lost Income..$

Medical Reports...$

GENERAL DAMAGES ....$

Total Demand...$

Include at the end of your **demand letter**. See next section.

<u>Negotiating Your Settlement</u>

It is important for you to decide on the <u>minimum value</u> of your claim <u>before</u> approaching the Injury Claims Examiner with your demand letter.

As stated previously, the Injury Claims Examiner may try to make a quick or low offer. You should not accept this.

The key for you is to <u>know what your claim is really worth</u> and to substantiate the value of your claim with a breakdown of damages in your demand letter.

<u>Insurance Settlement Secret # 102</u>

Instead of being in a rush to settle your injury. Take your time. Wait a few months **after your have finished all your treatments** to make sure you really have recovered.

For a <u>Minor</u> injury claim you should wait a minimum of **3 months**.

For a <u>Small</u> injury Claim it is to your benefit to wait **6 months** before sending your settlement demand.

Also monitor the Statute of Limitations in your state.

Patience will pay off big time because you now know this puts real <u>pressure</u> on the Insurance Company.

Remember, if you hired a personal injury lawyer the settlement date will be delayed for another year at least, and maybe several years.

Final Steps

1. Gather all your medical and Income loss <u>documentation</u>

2. Calculate the value of your Injury claim according to the **Insurance Settlement Secrets^{TM} Formula** you learned in the previous section.

3. Write your Demand letter and include the Breakdown of what you are seeking.

On the next page is a SAMPLE DEMAND LETTER in the same format that personal injury lawyers use when they present their demand.

Date

Bodily Injury Examiner
At-fault Driver's insurance Company
Address

Dear Mr../Ms:

Re: Your Insured Driver: (At-Fault Driver's name)
Your file #:

Thank you for your letter/telephone call of (Date). (IF YOU RECEIVED LETTER OR PHONE CALL FROM THE AT FAULT INSURANCE COMPANY)

As you know I was injured in a motor vehicle accident caused by your insured driver on (Date of Accident).

The circumstances of the accident were (DESCRIBE ACCIDENT FROM JUST BEFORE IMPACT. REFER TO SECTION ON COMMON TYPES OF ACCIDENTS FOR MORE INFO)

As a result of the accident, (DESCRIBE IN <u>NARRATIVE FORM</u> AND GIVE PARAGRAPH FOR EACH HEADING.)

TELL **<u>YOUR STORY</u>** AND GIVE EXACT DETAILS.

DESCRIBE THE DAMAGES TO YOUR VEHICLE AND THE TOTAL COST TO REPAIR. IF THE AT-FAULT DRIVER'S INSURANCE COMPANY PAID YOU DIRECTLY OR REIMBURSED YOUR OWN INSURANCE COMPANY FOR THE DAMAGES, STATE THIS.

DESCRIBE HOW YOU FELT IMMEDIATELY AFTER THE ACCIDENT, THE PAIN , STIFFNESS, DIZZINESS, HEADACHES,

BLEEDING, TROUBLE SLEEPING ETC.

DESCRIBE MEDICAL TREATMENT RECEIVED: DESCRIBE FIRST VISIT TO HOSPITAL, YOUR COMPLAINTS, DOCTOR'S DIAGNOSIS AND RECOMMENDATIONS, MEDICATIONS RECEIVED, IF X-RAYS RECOMMENDED ETC.

(DESCRIBE DATE AND TIME OF VISIT TO FAMILY DOCTOR, YOUR COMPLAINTS, EXAMINATION FINDINGS, DIAGNOSIS AND TREATMENT RECOMMENDATIONS.

(DESCRIBE ALL VISITS TO TREATMENT CLINICS FOR PHYSIOTHERAPY, CHIROPRACTIC TREATMENTS, MASSAGE, ACUPUNCTURE, GYM PROGRAMS, HOME EXERCISE PROGRAMS, MEDICATIONS, MEDIAL EQUIPMENT SUCH AS COLLAR, CRUTCHES, T.E.N.S. MACHINE ETC.)

(DESCRIBE IF YOU WERE PUT OFF WORK, FOR HOW LONG AND HOW THIS HAS PUT YOU UNDER FINANCIAL STRAIN,

(DESCRIBE RETURN TO WORK AND ANY ONGOING PAIN AND AGGRAVATION AT WORK, OR IF YOU WILL HAVE TO FIND ANOTHER TYPE OF WORK, ACCORDING TO DOCTOR)

(DESCRIBE ANY FLARE-UPS OR SUBSEQUENT RE-AGGRAVATION OF YOUR INJURY AND MEDICAL ATTENTION YOU RECEIVED.)

(DESCRIBE LIFE DISRUPTION, INABILITY TO DO HOUSEKEEPING, LOOK AFTER KIDS, ATTEND SCHOOL COURSES, MISSED SOCIAL EVENTS SUCH AS BIRTHDAYS, GRADUATIONS OR WEDDINGS.)

(DESCRIBE LIMITS OR INABILITY TO PARTICIPATE IN RECREATIONAL ACTIVITIES.)

(DESCRIBE THE EMOTIONAL TOLL THIS WHOLE EXPERIENCE HAS TAKEN.)

(DESCRIBE ANY ONGOING DISCOMFORT)

(DESCRIBE ANY FUTURE EXPENSES YOU EXPECT FOR HOUSEKEEPING AND FUTURE CARE.)

Attached are: (LIST AND ATTACH ALL DOCUMENTATION YOU HAVE TO SUPPORT YOUR CLAIM, SUCH AS HOSPITAL EMERGENCY BILL, AMBULANCE RECEIPT, RECORD OF MEDICAL PAYMENTS RECEIVED THAT NEED TO BE REIMBURSED, LETTER /REPORT FROM YOUR DOCTOR, IF NOT ALREADY OBTAINED BY AT-FAULT INJURY EXAMINER, PHYSIO CLINIC, CHIROPRACTOR OR MASSAGE CLINIC REPORTS, LETTER FROM EMPLOYER DOCUMENTING WAGE LOSS, ETC.).

If you require further medical documentation other than provided, please advise.

(CONCLUSION)

As a result of this Motor vehicle accident caused by the negligence of your Insured and the resulting injury I suffered, I am seeking $ _____(Total Dollar amount of your claim).

(INCLUDE BREAKDOWN of FIGURES WITH DEMAND)

Special Damages:
Hospital Emergency.....................................$
Medical Payments Claim.......................... $
Income Loss..$
Loss of Housekeeping..............................$ ($1000-$1500
Future Care...$

General Damages ....$

Pre-Judgement Interest Generals..............$
Pre-Judgement Interest Specials..............$

Total...$_____

166

I hope to hear from you within the next 30 days to resolve this matter.

Sincerely,

(Your Name)

The Demand Letter is Your Story

As you see the Demand letter is simply a narrative of your STORY. This your chance to shine.

The more compelling your STORY the more pressure it puts on the Injury Claims Examiner, because he or she knows that if you ever do hire a lawyer and if this ever went to court, the Insurance Company could not win.

In the first part of the Demand letter make sure you reaffirm the key elements that their driver was the CAUSE of the motor vehicle accident and that you suffered an INJURY AS A RESULT.

Insurance Settlement Secret # 103

If the At-fault driver's Insurance Company paid you directly or reimbursed your Insurance Company for what they paid you for your vehicle damage repairs, state this in the letter to remind them they have accepted liability.

Insurance Settlement Tip # 19

Attach a copy of the damage appraisal, if you have it, or Invoice from the Body Repair Shop that repaired your vehicle.

This reinforces the fact that their driver was at fault and they cannot avoid paying settlement.

Insurance Settlement Secret # 104

Attach copies of all relevant Medical Documentation you have obtained:

The Emergency Record, a report from your Doctor and copies of Treatment Records from your Physiotherapy Clinic, Chiropractor or massage therapist, copies of receipts for medication and other out of pocket medical expenses.

If you are claiming other miscellaneous special damages, such as housekeeping costs, attach copies of receipts.

By attaching medical documentation your are reinforcing that your were INJURED AS A RESULT OF THE MOTOR VEHICLE ACCIDENT.

At the same time you are providing documentary evidence to support the Demand figures in the breakdown at the end of the Demand letter.

Make a copy of the Demand letter and send with the copies of documentation.

If you cannot afford or would prefer that the Injury Claims Examiner pays for and obtains the medical documentation from your Doctor and your Private Health Insurer or your own Insurer, you will need to have signed the Medical Authorization allowing the Injury Examiner to obtain this information.

Insurance Settlement Secret # 105

Also it is VERY IMPORTANT that you CONFIRM that the Injury Examiner has followed through and obtained the medical documentation, **before** you send your demand letter.

The demand letter is much more persuasive when the Injury Examiner has the supporting documentation right there in the file when he or she receives the demand letter.

Remember you have the option of obtaining the documentation yourself and attaching any invoices for these reports or records.

Insurance Settlement Secret # 106

Don't let the Injury Claims Examiner forget about your claim.

Request a specific date for the Examiner to respond and if the date comes around with no response call and leave a message with your **Name, Claim or File number** and **telephone number** with a gentle reminder.

Remember always to **be polite**. It pays big time.

If you are organized, calm, confident and polite it will show the Injury Claims Examiner that you know how the process works and that your claim is legitimate.

Keep calling and leaving telephone messages every 7 to 10 days gently reminding them who you are and for the Injury Examiner to respond to your Demand letter and quote the date the letter was sent.

You can be calm and polite because you KNOW exactly the STATUS of your claim. You know you are in the Negotiation Stage and that your claim is ROCK SOLID.

Eventually the Injury Claims Examiner will review your demand letter with the attached medical documentation.

Insurance Settlement Secret # 107

Most Injury Claims Examiners will be very impressed with you. In fact they will likely be very happy because you have actually done most of their work for them.

You have addressed each of the elements that they are looking for:

1. That their driver was LIABLE for the motor vehicle accident
2. You SUFFERED INJURIES AS A RESULT
3. You have provided the DOCUMENTATION to support and substantiate your Claim Demand.

Requesting More Medical Records

If the Injury Claims Examiner calls you seeking additional medical records, other than what you have provided do **not start negotiating** on the phone with them.

Insurance Settlement Secret # 108

Injury Claims Examiner have lots of experience negotiating claims.

By entering into negotiations you are showing your hand that you are anxious to get this settled. (Of course you are but don't let them know this.)

The Counter Offer

The Injury Claims Examiner will usually also state that they don't accept your figures and that they are unreasonable and unrealistic and then make you a much lower offer.

Insurance Settlement Secret # 109

Request that the Injury Claims Examiner respond in writing stating clearly their concerns and what further evidence is needed.

This is extra work for them. This forces the Injury Claims Examiner to sit down and really analyze your injury claim.

If you have followed through with all the steps in stages 1,2 and 3, your injury claim demand should be **"bullet proof"**.

The Injury Claims Examiner will have a <u>hard time finding any fault</u> with your claim demand.

If you receive a letter seeking some more documentation, and the request is reasonable, you may advise the Examiner that you will provide the records if the Insurance Company is willing to pay for them.

Keep calling and leaving telephone messages every 7 to 10 days gently reminding them who you are and for the Injury Examiner to respond to your Demand letter and quote the date the letter was sent.

Insurance Settlement Tip #21

Telephone messages are very powerful because the Injury Claims Examiner's voice-mailbox fills up every day with dozens of messages.

Than means he or she has to listen to them all, take notes, and do something.

YOU HAVE EVERY RIGHT TO DO THIS! YOU SUFFERED AN INJURY AS A RESULT OF A MOTOR VEHICLE ACCIDENT AND THE INSURANCE COMPANY IS LIABLE.

Insurance Settlement Secret # 110

Have PATIENCE. If you keep leaving messages, eventually the overworked and underpaid Injury Claims Examiner will have to make a DECISION on your injury claim.

He or she may call you again and try and bump up their offer.

HOLD FIRM -- TIME IS ON YOUR SIDE

1. Remember, the Insurance Company is **losing a lot of money** while your injury claim is open.

171

2. If you have followed all the steps your claim is **"bullet proof"**.

3. If you have added your Special Damages correctly and used the **Settlement Secret Formula**, you demand is **reasonable**.

Statute of Limitations

Monitor the <u>Statute of Limitation</u> period in your state or the state where the accident happened. Most states allow 2 or more years from the date of the accident.

If you live in one of the few States where the <u>Statute of Limitations</u> to bring an action is less than 2 years from the date of the accident and the deadline is approaching, write the following <u>letter</u> to the Injury Claims examiner:

Your Name
Your Address

Bodily Injury Examiner
At -fault Driver's Insurance Company Name
Address

Dear Mr./Ms:

  Re: Your Insured Driver: (At-Fault Driver's name)
      Your file #:

This letter is further to our telephone conversation and my Demand letter of____ (Date).

Please advise if _____(At-Fault Insurance Company Name) accepts my demand offer.

If I do not hear from you within the next____ days (7-14 days), you will leave me no choice but to obtain legal representation and file a summons and complaint with the court and arrange service of process on your Insured _____

(At-Fault Driver's name) and _____*(At-Fault Insurance Company Name)*

Sincerely,

Your Name

NOTE: The threat to commence a legal action at this stage is far more potent than just after the motor vehicle accident.

Your claim for damages for your injury as a result of the motor vehicle accident which was caused by their insured driver is not hypothetical. It is now VERY REAL.

The at-fault driver's Insurance Company now has all the **evidence** before them. The Injury Examiner knows that they are bound to pay because **you have addressed all their concerns**.

They also know if you hire a personal injury lawyer at this stage your file will remain open for much longer and they will likely have to hire Defense counsel and lose more money.

The **extra 30-40%** you built in to your general damages amount in your settlement demand looks perfectly reasonable. The Injury Examiner knows that they will have to pay this for legal costs any way.

If you have followed the steps through stages 1-3, your Injury Claim Demand letter and Documentation are **"bullet proof"**. The Insurance Company knows they cannot win in court.

Every day your injury claim is open the Insurance Company is **losing money**. The Injury Examiner has all the documentation he or she needs to substantiate agreeing to your settlement amount.

Eventually, just to get rid of you and **close the claim**, the overworked and underpaid Injury Claims Examiner will call you and **agree** to your demand amount.

Signing The Final Release
And Receiving your Settlement Check

The Injury Claims Examiner will then ISSUE A CHECK payable to You which will take a few business days to arrive at his or her desk.

A FINAL RELEASE will be drafted. See sample on the next page.

The Final Release will state words to the effect:

FINAL RELEASE

IN CONSIDERATION OF $_____ DOLLARS (the amount of the settlement check), payable to _____(Your Name)

You FOREVER DISCHARGE/RELEASE_____ (the NAME OF THE INSURED DRIVER(S) and _____(THE INSURANCE COMPANY) from all and any LIABILITY for BODILY INJURY as a result of the motor vehicle accident that occurred on _____(Date of Accident) at _____(location).

The release will usually include words stating:

IT IS UNDERSTOOD AND AGREED that this payment is in no way an ADMISSION of Liability on the part of NAME OF THE INSURED DRIVER(S) and (THE INSURANCE COMPANY)

_____   On the day ___of _____(Date)
Your Signature

_____
Witness Signature

The Insurance Company will either send you the Final Release to sign and return and send the check, or arrange to have their representative meet with your in person to **exchange the Final Release for your check**.

Auto Policy Limits.

In some states the amount of total liability coverage for bodily injury is quite low, such as $10,000 for an accident victim.

If the at-fault Injury Examiner argues that your damages demand exceeds their *"policy limits"* you will need to request from the Examiner that they put the policy limits in writing.

Your have two options in this case:

1. If you have "Under-insured" motorist coverage on your own insurance policy you can settle with the at-fault Insurance Company to their policy limits, and then pursue the remainder of your damages through your own insurance company's "Under -insurance" policy.

2. The other option is to contact a personal injury lawyer to determine the personal assets of the at-fault driver, beyond his or her insurance coverage.

This will help to determine whether it is worth pursuing the at-fault driver in a lawsuit.

LAST RESORT

Sometimes Insurance Companies Claims Departments let a file slip through the cracks, either through incompetence or staff changes.

If for some reason the At-Fault Driver's Insurance Company still refuses to agree to your settlement amount you have the option of last resort.

You can hire a personal injury lawyer. See next section.

Last Resort: Hire a Personal Injury Lawyer

All the steps you have taken in Stages 1 and 2 are exactly what a competent personal injury lawyer would advise you to do.

If you had hired a personal injury lawyer the day after your motor vehicle accident you would still have to do **all the same steps**.

Only you could go to the Hospital Emergency, visit your Doctor, open different claims, follow up on your treatment and take medication etc. No personal injury lawyer could do that for you.

The only difference is that if you hired a personal injury lawyer he or she would be seeking up to **30-40% of your injury settlement** from the Insurance Company.

By hiring a lawyer at this stage as a last resort, it is much harder for the personal injury lawyer to justify such high fees. You are in a **much better financial position**.

Also, if you monitored the Statue of Limitations period as advised, you have **not jeopardized any of your legal rights**.

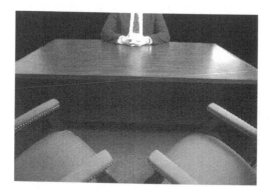

Hiring a Lawyer/ Attorney

Not all lawyers are good personal injury lawyers. Ask around through friends and colleagues or other lawyers who is the best personal injury lawyer in your community.

Many of the big name lawyers are known by reputation by the Insurance Companies.

Insurance Settlement Secret #111

Just because you consult with a lawyer does not mean that you have to hire a lawyer.

Verify with the lawyer if you can meet for a consultation, and confirm if the lawyer is willing to represent you on a **reduced fee arrangement**.

Bring copies of all your documents including your demand letter, Medical reports and records, expenses, income loss, and any correspondence between you and the Insurance Company.

Remember, you have done all the work here. You may be able to request that the lawyer draft a letter to the Insurance Company on your behalf.

Insurance Settlement Secret #112

It is common for there to be friction between the lawyer and the client over fees. It is important that you establish beforehand what the **fee arrangement** is with your lawyer.

Since you have done all the work, and have the supporting documentation you may be able to arrange a reduced fee structure by having the lawyer negotiate the settlement on your behalf for a prearranged hourly limit.

For any agreement with the lawyer about fees make sure you **get it in writing.**

At this stage, and with all the evidence you have gathered, a **simple**

letter or **phone call** from the lawyer should be enough to get the Insurance Company to agree to your settlement demand.

It is hard to imagine the Insurance Company wanting to incur any more expense on your injury claim.

If your lawyer files an action with the court and arranges service of papers on the at-fault driver, the Insurance Company will have to hire Defense Counsel or use in-house Defense Counsel.

If your injury claim reaches the stage where the Insurance Company has hired Defense counsel, the Defense counsel will ask the Insurance Company Injury Examiner for his or her file with all the documentation you have produced.

The Insurance Company Defense lawyer will also ask your lawyer to produce the documentation for your injury claim.

Once the Defense lawyer sees all the documentation you have produced he/she will likely advise the Insurance Company to accept your settlement demand.

Remember, you have ALREADY ADDRESSED each of the KEY elements that the at-fault driver's Insurance Company needed to confirm:

1. That their driver was LIABLE for CAUSING the motor vehicle accident .

2. You SUFFERED INJURIES AS A RESULT of the motor vehicle accident.

3. You have provided the DOCUMENTATION to support and substantiate your Injury Claim Demand.

If you have followed all the steps in Stages 1,2 and 3 your claim will be **"bullet proof"**.

If you calculated the value of your settlement demand according to the **Insurance Settlement Secret**^{TM} formula, then your demand is **reasonable** by Insurance Industry standards.

It is very unlikely that the Insurance Company Defense Counsel can in good faith advise the Insurance Company to proceed to trial.

Mediation

One other option if there is continued deadlock is to go to Mediation. Mediation is an alternative process for dispute resolution.

In Mediation the two sides sit down with a neutral Third Party who assists the parties reaching a mutually agreeable settlement.

Checklist - Stage 1

Immediate Steps you MUST take after a Motor Vehicle Accident.

- [ ] 1. Go to the **Hospital Emergency**.

- [ ] 2. **Write down** the MVA circumstances and your physical complaints.

- [ ] 3. **Read** your **Automobile Insurance Policy**.

- [ ] 4. **Call and notify your own Insurance Company** that you have been in an accident. Give insurance and contact information of the other driver.

- [ ] 5. Open a **Vehicle Damages claim** with your own Insurance Company if you have Collision coverage, even if *"only a scratch"*.

- [ ] 6. If injured, open a **Medical Payments** (or **Personal Injury Protection (PIP)** if in No Fault State) claim with your own Insurance Company.

- [ ] 7. If you have **Private Health Coverage** or other Health Insurance Coverage, open a claim with them.

- [ ] 8. Call and arrange an appointment with your **family doctor**.

- [ ] 9. When the **at-fault driver's Insurance Company** or their representative calls within days, confirm facts of the MVA and, if injured say *"Yes"*.

- [ ] 10. Open a **Vehicle Damages claim** with the At-Fault Insurance Company if you had no Collision coverage on your own Insurance Policy, even if *"only a scratch"* to your vehicle.

181

☐ 11. If you are in any way injured, **Open a Liability Injury claim** with the At-Fault Insurance Company unless in No-Fault State and are covered under PIP.

☐ 12. Record the Name of the At-Fault Insurance Company Injury Examiner, Mailing address, Contact info and also the **Claim or File #.**

☐ 13. Record the **date, time and subjects discussed** during the telephone conversation, **on the contact sheet**.

☐ 14. When you receive forms package from the at-fault Insurance Company: Fill out **Bodily Injury Questionnaire**. Use your discretion whether to sign Medical Authorization.

☐ 15. Write a **Confirmation letter** confirming the conversation and that you are opening a claim(s) for Injury and Vehicle damages (if no Collision coverage with your Insurance Company.)

☐ 16. **Make copies** of the forms and **send** what you sign back to at-fault driver's Insurance Company with **Confirmation letter**.

☐ 17. An Adjuster from y**our Insurance Company** may wish to meet with you for a **written statement**. You must cooperate with your own Insurance Company.

☐ 18. An Adjuster from the **at-fault driver's Insurance Company** may wish to meet with you for a statement. Use discretion. If you do sign, request copy of your statement.

Checklist Stage (2)

Medical Treatment & Rehabilitation

☐ 1. **Follow through with your treatment plan** recommended by your doctor. Attend all necessary therapeutic treatments.

☐ 2. **Write down** your complaints of pain and discomfort from your injury in **Medical Treatment log**. Document visits to treating Clinics and Doctors.

☐ 3. **Keep receipts** of all medical expenses.

☐ 4. If you have **no medical health coverage** through your insurance or through your employer, call or **send a letter** to at-fault Insurance Company Injury Examiner and **request that they cover treatments**. (See sample letter)

☐ 5. Monitor and **record** recovery in your **Medical Treatment Log.**

☐ 6. When complete treatment program, visit your family doctor again to **confirm full recovery.**

☐ 7. **Record** in your Medical Treatment log the **date of last visit to your doctor.**

☐ 8. If you recovery is slow, verify the Statute of Limitations period in your State.

☐ 9. If you are in a **No-Fault State and used up the limits of PIP** coverage but you feel your injury is more serious and you haven't been fully compensated, check the **Threshold** requirements in your State.

☐ 10. **Visit your doctor** again to see **if you meet the Impairment Threshold** requirements to pursue a liability claim in your No-Fault State.

☐ 11. If you meet the Threshold requirements, contact the At-Fault driver's Insurance Company and advise you wish to <u>Open an Liability Injury claim</u> .

Checklist Stage  3

Negotiation and Settlement Process

☐ 1. **Wait** a minimum of **3 - 6 months** after full recovery to confirm no relapse.

☐ 2. **Gather your supporting documentation**, receipts, Clinic treatment records, and invoices etc.

☐ 3. Call or write to the at-fault Insurance Company Injury Examiner and **confirm** if they will **pay for a medical report** from your doctor.

☐ 4. Once you have received confirmation, then **write to your doctor** for a **detailed medical report** describing your injuries as a result of the accident.

☐ 5. Write or obtain from your **Medical Payments** provider a **record of total treatments and expenses you received.** If required to **reimburse Medical Payments** from your Insurer, obtain **letter stating this amount.**

☐ 6. If you had **income loss**, obtain a letter from your Employer documenting loss of wages and time off.

☐ 7. Make **copies of all documentation** your receive.

☐ 8. **Calculate the Value of your injury claim** using the **Settlement Secrets Formula**TM.

☐ 9. Write your **demand letter**, including all details of your pain and suffering. Refer to your Medical Treatment log.

☐ 10. **Send your demand letter and attach copies** of your medical and income loss documentation. Also attach the Invoices for the Medical Reports.

☐ 11. If you **have not heard** from the Injury Examiner by 14 days, **call and leave message.** Repeat process every 7-10 days

☐ 12. When at-fault Insurance Company Injury Examiner calls and advises you that they will not accept your settlement demand, **do not negotiate on the phone.** Request that the Injury Examiner write a **letter stating their counter-offer** and **giving detailed reasons.**

☐ 13. If you **have not heard** from the Injury Examiner, **call again** and leave message. Repeat process every 7-10 days

☐ 14. Review **counteroffer letter** If there is missing documentation and it is reasonable, obtain this documentation yourself or have the at-fault Insurance Company Injury Examiner obtain this information.

☐ 15. Call the Injury Examiner and **confirm** whether he or she has **received the missing documentation.**

☐ 16. If the **Injury Examiner still refuses to accept your settlement demand**, write another letter stating that your **demand still stands** and if it is not accepted within 30 days, you will obtain legal counsel.

☐ 17. **Wait and be patient** for developments.

☐ 18. If you haven't heard from the at-fault Insurance Company Examiner after thirty days, call and **leave messages every 7-10 days**, until you receive a response.

☐ 19. If the **Injury Examiner still refuses** to accept your injury demand, call and **request the name of the Supervisor.**

☐ 20. Send same **letter to the <u>Supervisor</u>** stating that your **demand still stands** and if it is not accepted within 14 days, you will obtain legal counsel and file a Notice of Action.

☐ 21. If you don't hear by set date, call and **leave messages every 7-10 days**, until you receive a response.

☐ 22. When the Injury Examiner finally calls and accepts your demand, arrange a time and place to **exchange the check and sign the final release**.

☐ 23. If the at-fault Insurer Injury Examiner advises you that your **demand exceeds their policy limits**, request that they **confirm that in writing**.

☐ 24. If you are within a month from the Statute of Limitation period, and the at fault driver's Insurance Company **still refuses to accept your demand**, at this point **contact a personal injury lawyer**.

Stage

Vehicle Damages Claim Contact Sheet

File No:_____
Policy : _____   Date of MVA_____
Insurance Company _____
Vehicle Damages Adjuster name:_____
Insurance Company Address_____
_____ _____ ____

Tel.: _____Ext: _____ Fax _____
Date You Reported Accident: _____/____/_____
Time: _____
Location of Loss_____
Circumstances:_____
_____
_____
_____
_____
_____
_____
_____
_____
_____
_____

Describe Your Vehicle Damages _____
_____
_____

Where Your Vehicle is Visible: _____
Total Damages stated by Appraiser $_____
Your Deductible $_____
Payment Received for Your Vehicle Damages $_____

Note: If you have No Collision coverage with your Insurer, you must claim your vehicle damages against At-Fault Driver's Insurance Company. The Process is almost the same.

<u>Stage</u>

<u>Medical Payments, or PIP Claim Contact Sheet</u>

File No:_____
Policy : _____ Date of MVA_____
Insurance Company _____
Medical Payments Adjuster name:_____
Insurance Company Address_____
_____

Tel.: _____ Ext. _____ Fax _____
E-mail: _____

Contact Date: _____/_____/_____
Record of Conversation: _____
_____
_____
_____

Contact Date: _____/_____/_____
Record of Conversation: _____
_____
_____
_____

Contact Date: _____/_____/_____
Record of Conversation: _____
_____
_____
_____

Contact Date: _____/_____/_____
Record of Conversation: _____
_____
_____
_____
_____
_____

Stage  1 2

Private/ Employer Health Insurance Claim

File No:_____
Policy : _____
Health Insurance Company : _____
Health Claim Analyst name:_____
Health Insurance Company Address_____
_____
_____
Tel.: _____ Ext. _____ Fax _____
E-mail: _____
Contact Date: _____/_____/_____
Record of Conversation: _____
_____
_____
_____

Contact Date: _____/_____/_____
Record of Conversation: _____
_____
_____
_____

Contact Date: _____/_____/_____
Record of Conversation: _____
_____
_____
_____

Contact Date: _____/_____/_____
Record of Conversation: _____
_____
_____
_____
_____

Stages

Sample Medical and Wage Authorizations

(Sample) AUTHORIZATION FOR MEDICAL INFORMATION

Date_____

This will authorize you to disclose to _____
Insurance Company or its representative, any and all information you may have regarding my condition while under your observation or treatment at any time, including medical history and findings; consultation, prescriptions, treatment, x-ray, special consultation reports, diagnosis and prognosis, and copies of all hospital and medical records.
Signed_____
Address_____

_____ _____ _____

(Sample) AUTHORIZATION FOR WAGE INFORMATION

Date_____

This form or a copy will authorize you to give_____
Insurance Company or its representative, all information in your possession regarding my rate of pay, amount of overtime, commissions, vacation allowance, nature of my employment, time lost from work and other information which they may require.
Signed_____
Address_____

_____ _____ _____

<u>Stage</u> 1 2 3
<u>Liability Injury Claim Contact Sheet</u>

Name of At-Fault Driver_____

At-Fault Driver's
Insurance Company _____

Injury Examiner Name:_____

Claim #_____

At-Fault Driver's Insurance Company Address

_____

_____

Tel.: _____ Ext. _____ Fax _____

E-mail: _____

Contact Date: _____/_____/_____

Record of Conversation: _____

_____

_____

Contact Date: _____/_____/_____

Record of Conversation: _____

_____

Contact Date: _____/_____/_____

Record of Conversation: _____

_____

Contact Date: _____/_____/_____

Record of Conversation: _____

_____

_____

_____

Contact Date: _____/_____/_____
Record of Conversation: _____
_____
_____
_____

Contact Date: _____/_____/_____
Record of Conversation: _____
_____
_____
_____

Contact Date: _____/_____/_____
Record of Conversation: _____
_____
_____
_____

Contact Date: _____/_____/_____
Record of Conversation: _____
_____
_____
_____
_____

Contact Date: _____/_____/_____
Record of Conversation: _____
_____
_____
_____

Contact Date: _____/_____/_____
Record of Conversation: _____
_____
_____
_____
_____

Stage 1
Medical Treatment Logs

Hospital Emergency:
By Ambulance ( ) Yes ( ) No
Date: _____ Time: _____am ( ) pm ( )
Your Complaints:_____
_____
_____
_____
_____
_____
_____
_____
_____

Hospital Attending Doctor: _____
Doctor's diagnosis:_____
_____
Treatment Prescribed: _____
_____
_____

X-Rays: Yes ( ) No ( )
Medication: _____
Physiotherapy: yes ( ) No ( )
Chiropractor: yes ( ) No ( )
Massage : Yes ( ) No ( )
Other:_____
Prognosis: _____
_____
_____
_____
_____

__Stage__ 1

First Visit to Family/ Treating Doctor:

Date: _____ Time: _____am ( ) pm ( )
Your Complaints:_____

_____

_____

_____

_____

_____

_____

Doctor name:_____
Doctor's diagnosis:_____
Treatment Prescribed:_____

_____

_____

Referred to X-Rays: Yes ( ) No ( )
Medication: _____
Physiotherapy: yes ( ) No ( )
Chiropractor: yes ( ) No ( )
Massage : Yes ( ) No ( )
Other:_____

Put Off work: Yes ( ) No ( )
Estimated Return to Work Date _____
Prognosis: _____

_____

_____

_____

_____

_____

_____

_____

Stage ②
Ongoing Medical Treatment Log

Date: _____
Clinic Name: _____
Your Complaints:_____
_____
_____
_____

Treatments Received: _____
_____

Date: _____
Clinic Name: _____
Your Complaints:_____
_____
_____
_____

Treatments Received: _____
_____

Date: _____
Clinic Name: _____
Your Complaints:_____
_____
_____
_____

Treatments Received: _____
_____

Date: _____
Clinic Name: _____
Your Complaints:_____
_____
_____
_____

Treatments Received: _____
_____
_____
_____

<u>Stage</u> ②
<u>Follow up Visits to Family or Treating Doctor:</u>

Date: _____
Your Complaints:_____
_____
_____

Doctor's diagnosis:_____
Treatment Prescribed: _____
_____

Prognosis: _____

Date: _____
Your Complaints:_____
_____
_____

Doctor's diagnosis:_____
Treatment Prescribed: _____
_____

Prognosis: _____

Date: _____
Your Complaints:_____
_____
_____

Doctor's diagnosis:_____
Treatment Prescribed: _____
_____

Prognosis: _____

Date: _____
Your Complaints:_____
_____
_____
_____
Doctor's diagnosis:_____
Treatment Prescribed: _____
_____
_____
_____
Prognosis: _____

Date: _____
Your Complaints:_____
_____
_____
_____
Doctor's diagnosis:_____
Treatment Prescribed: _____
_____
_____
_____
Prognosis: _____

Date: _____
Your Complaints:_____
_____
_____
_____
Doctor's diagnosis:_____
Treatment Prescribed: _____
_____
_____
_____
Prognosis: _____

Stage ②

Medical Clinic Treatment Log

Date	Clinic	Complaints	Treatments

Mini Guide to State Legislation & Limits

Alabama
Required coverage types: bodily injury and property damage liability
Minimum liability limits: 20/40/10
No fault? no

Alaska
Required coverage types: bodily injury and property damage liability
Minimum liability limits: 50/100/25
No fault? no

Arizona
Required coverage types: bodily injury and property damage liability
Minimum liability limits: 15/30/10
No fault? no

Arkansas
Required coverage types: bodily injury and property damage liability
Minimum liability limits: 25/50/25
No fault? no

California
Required coverage types: bodily injury and property damage liability
Minimum liability limits: 15/30/5
No fault? no

Colorado
Required coverage types: bodily injury and property damage liability
Minimum liability limits: 25/50/15
No fault? no

Connecticut
Required coverage types: bodily injury and property damage liability, uninsured motorist
Minimum liability limits: 20/40/10
No fault? no

Delaware
Required coverage types: bodily injury and property damage liability, personal injury protection
Minimum liability limits: 15/30/10
No fault? no

DC
Required coverage types: bodily injury and property damage liability, uninsured motorist
Minimum liability limits: 25/50/10
No fault? yes

Florida
Required coverage types: property damage liability, personal injury protection
Minimum liability limits: 10/20/10
No fault? yes

Georgia
Required coverage types: bodily injury and property damage liability
Minimum liability limits: 25/50/25
No fault? no

Hawaii
Required coverage types: bodily injury and property damage liability, personal injury protection
Minimum liability limits: 20/40/10
No fault? yes

Idaho
Required coverage types: bodily injury and property damage liability
Minimum liability limits: 25/50/15
No fault? no

Illinois
Required coverage types: bodily injury and property damage liability, uninsured motorist
Minimum liability limits: 20/40/15
No fault? no

Indiana
Required coverage types: bodily injury and property damage liability
Minimum liability limits: 25/50/10
No fault? no

Iowa
Required coverage types: bodily injury and property damage liability
Minimum liability limits: 20/40/15
No fault? no

Kansas
Required coverage types: bodily injury and property damage liability, personal injury protection
Minimum liability limits: 25/50/10
No fault? yes

Kentucky
Required coverage types: bodily injury and property damage liability, personal injury protection
Minimum liability limits: 25/50/10
No fault? yes

Louisiana
Required coverage types: bodily injury and property damage liability
Minimum liability limits: 10/20/10
No fault? no

Maine
Required coverage types: bodily injury and property damage liability, uninsured motorist
Minimum liability limits: 50/100/25
No fault? no

Maryland
Required coverage types: bodily injury and property damage liability, uninsured and under-insured motorist
Minimum liability limits: 20/40/15
No fault? no

Massachusetts
Required coverage types: bodily injury and property damage liability, personal injury protection, uninsured motorist
Minimum liability limits: 20/40/5
No fault? yes

Michigan
Required coverage types: bodily injury and property damage liability, personal injury protection
Minimum liability limits: 20/40/10
No fault? yes

Minnesota
Required coverage types: bodily injury and property damage liability, personal injury protection, uninsured and under-insured motorist
Minimum liability limits: 30/60/10
No fault? yes

Mississippi
Required coverage types: bodily injury and property damage liability
Minimum liability limits: 10/20/5
No fault? no

Missouri
Required coverage types: bodily injury and property damage liability, uninsured motorist
Minimum liability limits: 25/50/10
No fault? no

Montana
Required coverage types: bodily injury and property damage liability
Minimum liability limits: 25/50/10
No fault? no

Nebraska
Required coverage types: bodily injury and property damage liability, uninsured and under-insured motorist
Minimum liability limits: 25/50/25
No fault? no

Nevada
Required coverage types: bodily injury and property damage liability
Minimum liability limits: 15/30/10
No fault? no

New Hampshire
Required coverage types: proof of financial responsibility, medical payments, uninsured motorist
Minimum liability limits: 25/50/25
No fault? no

New Jersey
Required coverage types: bodily injury and property damage liability, personal injury protection, uninsured motorist
Minimum liability limits: 15/30/5
No fault? yes

New Mexico
Required coverage types: bodily injury and property damage liability
Minimum liability limits: 25/50/10
No fault? no

New York
Required coverage types: bodily injury and property damage liability, uninsured motorist, personal injury protection
Minimum liability limits: 25/50/10
No fault? yes

North Carolina
Required coverage types: bodily injury and property damage liability
Minimum liability limits: 30/60/25
No fault? no

North Dakota
Required coverage types: bodily injury and property damage liability, personal injury protection, uninsured and under-insured motorist
Minimum liability limits: 25/50/25
No fault? yes

Ohio
Required coverage types: bodily injury and property damage liability
Minimum liability limits: 12.5/25/7.5
No fault? no

Oklahoma
Required coverage types: bodily injury and property damage liability
Minimum liability limits: 10/20/10
No fault? no

Oregon
Required coverage types: bodily injury and property damage liability, personal injury protection, uninsured and under-insured motorist
Minimum liability limits: 25/50/10
No fault? no

Pennsylvania
Required coverage types: bodily injury and property damage liability, medical payments
Minimum liability limits: 15/30/5
No fault? yes

Rhode Island
Required coverage types: bodily injury and property damage liability
Minimum liability limits: 25/50/25
No fault? no

South Carolina
Required coverage types: bodily injury and property damage liability, uninsured motorist
Minimum liability limits: 15/30/10
No fault? no

South Dakota
Required coverage types: bodily injury and property damage liability, uninsured motorist
Minimum liability limits: 25/50/25
No fault? no

Tennessee
Required coverage types: proof of financial responsibility
Minimum liability limits: 25/50/10
No fault? no

Texas
Required coverage types: bodily injury and property damage liability
Minimum liability limits: 20/40/15
No fault? no

Utah
Required coverage types: bodily injury and property damage liability, personal injury protection, uninsured and under-insured motorist
Minimum liability limits: 25/50/15
No fault? yes

Vermont
Required coverage types: bodily injury and property damage liability, uninsured motorist
Minimum liability limits: 25/50/10
No fault? no

Virginia
Required coverage types: bodily injury and property damage liability, uninsured and under-insured motorist
Minimum liability limits: 25/50/20
No fault? no

Washington
Required coverage types: bodily injury and property damage liability
Minimum liability limits: 25/50/10
No fault? no

West Virginia
Required coverage types: bodily injury and property damage liability, uninsured motorist
Minimum liability limits: 20/40/10
No fault? no

Wisconsin
Required coverage types: proof of financial responsibility, uninsured motorist
Minimum liability limits: 25/50/10
No fault? no

Wyoming
Required coverage types: bodily injury and property damage liability
Minimum liability limits: 25/50/20
No fault? no

Note: This is only a guide. State Insurance Legislation and Regulations change frequently. Check with your own Insurance Company, your Policy and your State Department of Insurance for current Coverage and Limits Requirements.

Sample letter: Open Liability Claim Confirmation

Your Name
Your Address

Bodily Injury Examiner   Date
At -fault Driver's Insurance Company
Address

Dear Mr./Ms:

Re: Your Insured Driver: (At-Fault Driver's name)
Your file #:

Further to our telephone conversation, this is to confirm I was injured in a motor vehicle accident with your insured driver on (Date of Accident).

The circumstances of the accident were

(DESCRIBE ACCIDENT FROM JUST BEFORE IMPACT.
 - SEE COMMON TYPES OF ACCIDENTS FOR MORE INFO)

As a result of the accident I was injured and am presently undergoing medical treatment.

This is notice that I wish to proceed with a Bodily Injury claim against (NAME OF AT-FAULT DRIVER'S INSURANCE COMPANY).

Please provide details of the Policy limits coverage of your Insured driver for Bodily Injury and Vehicle Damages Liability.

I will provide you will medical documentation once I have fully recovered from my injury.

Sincerely,

Your Name

Sample Letter: Medical Payment Request

Your Name
Your Address

Bodily Injury Examiner
At -fault Driver's Insurance Company
Address

Date

Dear Mr./Ms:

Re: Your Insured Driver: (At-Fault Driver's name)
Your file #:

This letter is further to our telephone conversation and my letter of (Date) confirming that I was injured in an accident with your insured driver.

As a result of my injury I have been referred by Dr._____ for ___ number of treatments at the _____ _____Clinic. Also I have been recommended to take _____ medication. Attached is a copy of the referral notes.

I confirm that I have no Private Health coverage and have no Medical Payments coverage through my own Automobile Insurance Company.

Please advise if _____ (NAME OF AT FAULT DRIVER'S INSURANCE COMPANY) would be prepared to cover the costs of the recommended treatment.

Without the recommended treatment my injury may be prolonged or become worse. Please respond as soon as possible.

Sincerely,

Your Name

Sample Demand Letter for Injury Settlement

Your Name
Your Address
Your Telephone #
Other contact Information

Date

Bodily Injury Examiner
At -fault Driver's Insurance Company
Address

Dear Mr./Ms:

> **Re: Your Insured Driver: (At-Fault Driver's name)**
> **Your file #:**

Thank you for you letter/ telephone call of (Date). (IF YOUR RECEIVED LETTER OR PHONE CALL FROM THE AT FAULT INSURANCE COMPANY)

As you know I was injured in a motor vehicle accident caused by your insured driver on (Date of Accident).

The circumstances of the accident were (DESCRIBE ACCIDENT FROM JUST BEFORE IMPACT. SEE TYPES OF ACCIDENTS FOR MORE INFO)

As a result of the accident, (DESCRIBE IN <u>NARRATIVE FORM</u> AND GIVE PARAGRAPH FOR EACH HEADING. TELL **YOUR STORY** AND GIVE EXACT DETAILS)

(HOW YOU FELT IMMEDIATELY AFTER THE ACCIDENT, PAIN, STIFFNESS, DIZZINESS, HEADACHES, BLEEDING, TROUBLE SLEEPING ETC.)

(MEDICAL TREATMENT RECEIVED: DESCRIBE FIRST VISIT TO HOSPITAL, YOUR COMPLAINTS, DOCTOR'S DIAGNOSIS AND RECOMMENDATIONS, MEDICATIONS RECEIVED, IF X-RAYS RECOMMENDED ETC.)

(DESCRIBE DATE AND TIME OF VISIT TO FAMILY DOCTOR, YOUR COMPLAINTS, EXAMINATION FINDINGS, DIAGNOSIS AND TREATMENT RECOMMENDATIONS.

(DESCRIBE ALL VISITS TO TREATMENT CLINICS FOR PHYSIOTHERAPY, CHIROPRACTIC TREATMENTS, MASSAGE, ACUPUNCTURE, GYM PROGRAMS, HOME EXERCISE PROGRAMS, MEDICATIONS, MEDIAL EQUIPMENT SUCH AS COLLAR, CRUTCHES, T.E.N.S. MACHINE ETC.)

(DESCRIBE IF YOU WERE PUT OFF WORK, FOR HOW LONG AND HOW THIS HAS PUT YOU UNDER FINANCIAL STRAIN,

(DESCRIBE RETURN TO WORK AND ANY ONGOING PAIN AND AGGRAVATION AT WORK, OR IF YOU WILL HAVE TO FIND ANOTHER TYPE OF WORK. (ACCORDING TO DOCTOR)

(DESCRIBE ANY FLARE-UPS OR SUBSEQUENT RE-AGGRAVATION OF YOUR INJURY AND MEDICAL ATTENTION YOU RECEIVED.)

(DESCRIBE LIFE DISRUPTION, INABILITY TO DO HOUSEKEEPING, LOOK AFTER KIDS, ATTEND SCHOOL COURSES, MISSED SOCIAL EVENTS SUCH AS BIRTHDAYS, GRADUATIONS OR WEDDINGS.)

(DESCRIBE LIMITS OR INABILITY TO PARTICIPATE IN RECREATIONAL ACTIVITIES.)

(DESCRIBE, THE EMOTIONAL TOLL THIS WHOLE EXPERIENCE HAS TAKEN.)

(DESCRIBE ANY ONGOING DISCOMFORT)

(DESCRIBE ANY FUTURE EXPENSES YOU EXPECT FOR HOUSEKEEPING AND FUTURE CARE.)

Attached are: (LIST AND ATTACH ALL DOCUMENTATION YOU HAVE TO SUPPORT YOUR CLAIM, SUCH AS HOSPITAL EMERGENCY BILL, AMBULANCE RECEIPT, RECORD OF MEDICAL PAYMENTS RECEIVED THAT NEED TO BE REIMBURSED, LETTER /REPORT FROM YOUR DOCTOR IF NOT ALREADY OBTAINED BY AT-FAULT INJURY EXAMINER, LETTER FROM EMPLOYER DOCUMENTING WAGE LOSS, ETC.

If you require further medical documentation other than provided, please advise.

(CONCLUSION AND BREAKDOWN OF DEMAND FIGURES)

As a result of this Motor vehicle accident caused by the negligence of your Insured and the resulting injury I suffered, I am seeking $ _____(Total Dollar amount of your claim) in damages.

Special Damages:
Hospital Emergency..$
Medical Payments Claim............................. $
General Damages *.. $*
Income Loss..$
Loss of Housekeeping..................................$ ($1000-$1500
Future Care...$
Prejudgement Interest Generals...................$
Prejudgement Interest Specials....................$

Total...$_____

I hope to hear from you within the next 30 days to resolve this matter.

Sincerely,

Your Name

Sample Letter: Threat of Legal Action

Your Name
Your Address

Your Telephone #
Other contact Information

Date

Bodily Injury Examiner
At -fault Driver's Insurance Company
Address

Dear Mr./Ms:

> **Re: Your Insured Driver: (At-Fault Driver's name)**
> **Your file #:**

This letter is further to our telephone conversation and my Demand letter of_____ (Date).

Please advise if _____(At Fault Insurance Company Name) accepts my demand offer.

If I do not hear from you within the next__ days (7-14 days), you will leave me no choice but to obtain legal representation and file a legal action with the court and arrange service of process against your Insured _____ (At-Fault Driver's name) and _____(At Fault Insurance Company Name)

Sincerely,

Your Name

25782451R00122

Made in the USA
San Bernardino, CA
11 November 2015